Ron Holt

ESSENTIALS

AQA
GCSE Physics
Revision Guide

Contents

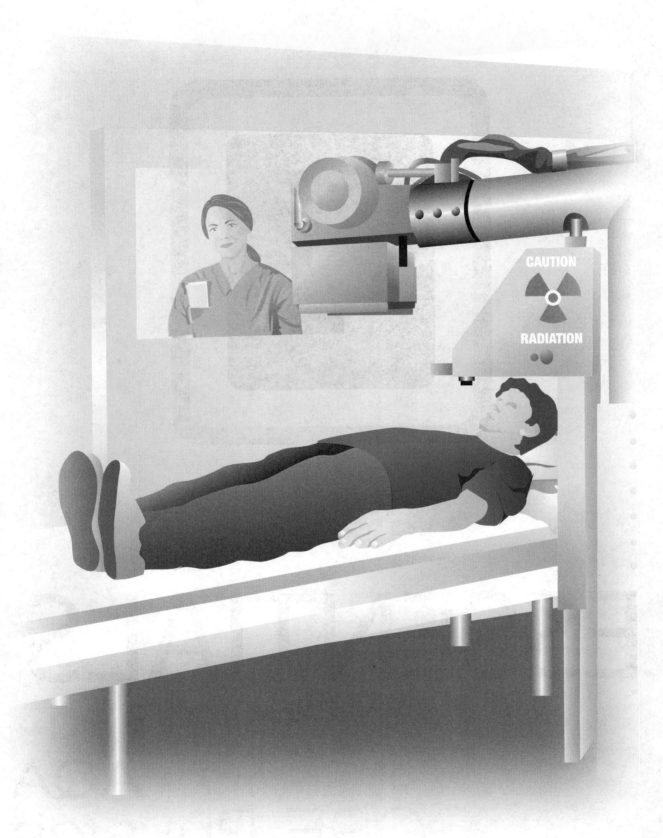

Contents

*N.B. The numbers in brackets correspond to the reference numbers
on the AQA GCSE Physics specification*

How Science Works – Explanation

The AQA GCSE Physics specification incorporates:

- **Science Content** – all the scientific explanations and evidence that you need to know for the exams. (It is covered on pages 12–65 of this revision guide.)
- **How Science Works** – a set of key concepts, relevant to all areas of science. It covers…
  - the relationship between scientific evidence, and scientific explanations and theories
  - how scientific evidence is collected
  - how reliable and valid scientific evidence is
  - the role of science in society
  - the impact science has on our lives
  - how decisions are made about the ways science and technology are used in different situations, and the factors affecting these decisions.

Your teacher(s) will have taught these two types of content together in your science lessons. Likewise, the questions on your exam papers will probably combine elements from both types of content. So, to answer them, you'll need to recall and apply the relevant scientific facts and knowledge of how science works.

The key concepts of How Science Works are summarised in this section of the revision guide (pages 5–11). You should be familiar with all of these concepts. If there is anything you are unsure about, ask your teacher to explain it to you.

How Science Works is designed to help you learn about and understand the practical side of science. It aims to help you develop your skills when it comes to…

- evaluating information
- developing arguments
- drawing conclusions.

The Thinking Behind Science

Science attempts to explain the world we live in.

Scientists carry out investigations and collect evidence in order to…

- **explain phenomena** (i.e. how and why things happen)
- **solve problems** using evidence.

Scientific knowledge and understanding can lead to the **development of new technologies** (e.g. in medicine and industry), which have a huge impact on **society** and the **environment**.

The Purpose of Evidence

Scientific evidence provides **facts** that help to answer a specific question and either **support** or **disprove** an idea or theory. Evidence is often based on data that has been collected through **observations** and **measurements**.

To allow scientists to reach conclusions, evidence must be…

- **repeatable** – other people should be able to repeat the same process
- **reproducible** – other people should be able to reproduce the same results
- **valid** – it must be repeatable, reproducible and answer the question.

N.B. If data isn't repeatable and reproducible, it can't be valid.

To ensure scientific evidence is repeatable, reproducible and valid, scientists look at ideas relating to…

- observations
- investigations
- measurements
- data presentation
- conclusions and evaluation.

How Science Works Overview

Observations

Most scientific investigations begin with an **observation**. A scientist observes an event or phenomenon and decides to find out more about how and why it happens.

The first step is to develop a **hypothesis**, which suggests an explanation for the phenomenon. Hypotheses normally suggest a relationship between two or more **variables** (factors that change).

Hypotheses are based on...

- careful observations
- existing scientific knowledge
- some creative thinking.

The hypothesis is used to make a **prediction**, which can be tested through scientific investigation. The data collected from the investigation will...

- support the hypothesis **or**
- show it to be untrue (refute it) **or**
- lead to the modification of the original hypothesis or the development of a new hypothesis.

If the hypothesis and models we have available to us do not completely match our data or observations, we need to check the validity of our observations or data, or amend the models.

Sometimes, if the new observations and data are valid, existing theories and explanations have to be revised or amended, and so scientific knowledge grows and develops.

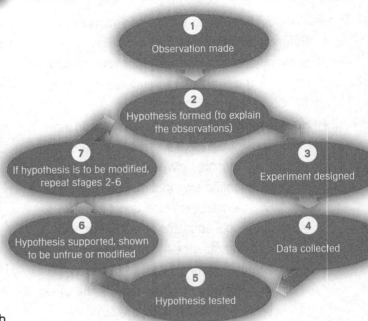

1. Observation made
2. Hypothesis formed (to explain the observations)
3. Experiment designed
4. Data collected
5. Hypothesis tested
6. Hypothesis supported, shown to be untrue or modified
7. If hypothesis is to be modified, repeat stages 2-6

Example

- Two scientists **observe** that freshwater shrimp are only found in certain parts of a stream.
- They use scientific knowledge of shrimp and water flow to develop a **hypothesis**, which relates the presence of shrimp (dependent variable) to the rate of water flow (independent variable). For example, a hypothesis could be: the faster the water flows, the fewer shrimp are found.
- They **predict** that shrimp are only found in parts of the stream where the water flow rate is below a certain value.
- They **investigate** by counting and recording the number of shrimp in different parts of the stream, where water flow rates differ.
- The **data** shows that more shrimp are present in parts of the stream where the flow rate is below a certain value. So, the data **supports** the hypothesis. But, it also shows that shrimp aren't always present in these parts of the stream.
- The scientists realise there must be another factor affecting the distribution of shrimp. They **refine their hypothesis**.

Investigations

An **investigation** involves collecting data to find out whether there is a relationship between two **variables**. A variable is a factor that can take different values.

In an investigation there are two types of variables:

- **Independent** variable – can be changed by the person carrying out the investigation. For example, the amount of water a plant receives.
- **Dependent** variable – measured each time a change is made to the independent variable, to see if it also changes. For example, the growth of the plant (measured by recording the number of leaves).

For a measurement to be valid it must measure only the appropriate variable.

Variables can have different types of values:

- **Continuous variables** – can take any numerical value (including decimals). These are usually measurements, e.g. temperature.
- **Categoric variables** – a variable described by a label, usually a word, e.g. different breeds of dog or blood group.
    - **Discrete variables** – only take whole-number values. These are usually quantities, e.g. the number of shrimp in a stream.
    - **Ordered variables** – have relative values, e.g. 'small', 'medium' or 'large'.

N.B. Numerical values, such as continuous variables, tend to be more informative than ordered and categoric variables.

An investigation tries to find out whether an **observed** link between two variables is…

- **causal** – a change in one variable causes a change in the other, e.g. the more cigarettes you smoke, the greater the chance that you will develop lung cancer.
- **due to association** – the changes in the two variables are linked by a third variable, e.g. as grassland decreases, the number of predators decreases (caused by a third variable, i.e. the number of prey decreasing).
- **due to chance** – the change in the two variables is unrelated; it is coincidental, e.g. people who eat more cheese than others watch more television.

Controlling Variables

In a **fair test**, the only factor that should affect the dependent variable is the independent variable. Other **outside variables** that could influence the results are kept the same, i.e. constant (control variables) or eliminated.

It's a lot easier to control all the other variables in a laboratory than in the field, where conditions can't always be controlled. The impact of an outside variable (e.g. light intensity or rainfall) has to be reduced by ensuring all the measurements are affected by it in the same way. For example, all the measurements should be taken at the same time of day.

Control groups are often used in biological and medical research to make sure that any observed results are due to changes in the independent variable only.

A sample is chosen that 'matches' the test group as closely as possible except for the variable that is being investigated, e.g. testing the effect of a drug on reducing blood pressure. The control group must be the same age, gender, have similar diets, lifestyles, blood pressure, general health, etc.

How Science Works Overview

Accuracy and Precision

How accurate data needs to be depends on what the investigation is trying to find out. For example, when measuring the volume of acid needed to neutralise an alkaline solution it is important that equipment is used that is able to accurately measure volumes of liquids.

The data collected must be **precise** enough to form a **valid conclusion**: it should provide clear evidence for or against the hypothesis.

Measurements

Apart from control variables, there are a number of factors that can affect the reliability and validity of measurements:

- **Accuracy of instruments** – depends on how accurately the instrument has been calibrated. An accurate measurement is one that is close to the true value.
- **Resolution (or sensitivity) of instruments** – determined by the smallest change in value that the instrument can detect. The more sensitive the instrument, the more **precise** the value. For example, bathroom scales aren't sensitive enough to detect changes in a baby's mass, but the scales used by a midwife are.
- **Human error** – even if an instrument is used correctly, human error can produce random differences in repeated readings or a systematic shift from the true value if you lose concentration or make the same mistake repeatedly.
- **Systematic error** – can result from repeatedly carrying out the process incorrectly, making the same mistake each time.
- **Random error** – can result from carrying out a process incorrectly on odd occasions or by fluctuations in a reading. The smaller the random error the greater the accuracy of the reading.

To ensure data is as accurate as possible, you can…

- calculate the **mean** (average) of a set of repeated measurements to reduce the effect of random errors
- increase the number of measurements taken to improve the reliability of the mean / spot anomalies.

Preliminary Investigations

A trial run of an investigation will help identify appropriate values to be recorded, such as the number of repeated readings needed and their range and interval.

You need to examine any **anomalous** (irregular) values to try to determine why they appear. If they have been caused by equipment failure or human error, it is common practice to ignore them and not use them in any calculations.

There will always be some variation in the actual value of a variable, no matter how hard we try to repeat an event.

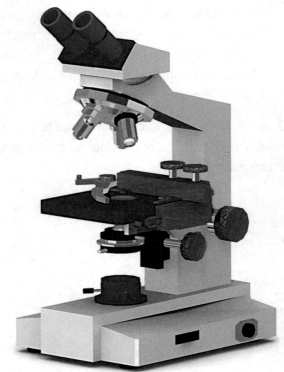

Presenting Data

Data is often presented in a **chart** or **graph** because it makes...

- any patterns more obvious
- it easier to see the relationship between two variables.

The **mean** (or average) of data is calculated by adding all the measurements together, then dividing by the number of measurements taken:

$$\text{Mean} = \frac{\text{Sum of all Values}}{\text{Number of Values}}$$

If you present data clearly, it is easier to identify any anomalous (irregular) values. The type of chart or graph you use to present data depends on the type of variable involved:

1 **Tables** organise data (but patterns and anomalies aren't always obvious)

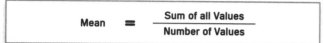

Height of student (cm)	127	165	149	147	155	161	154	138	145
Shoe size	5	8	5	6	5	5	6	4	5

2 **Bar charts** display data when the independent variable is categoric or discrete and the dependent variable is continuous.

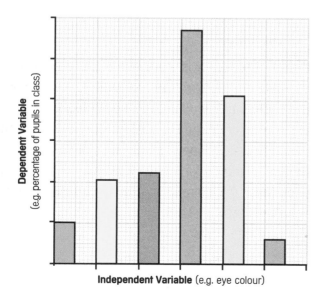

3 **Line graphs** display data when both variables are continuous.

- Points are joined by straight lines if you don't have data to support the values between the points.
- A line of best fit is drawn if there is sufficient data or if a trend can be assumed.

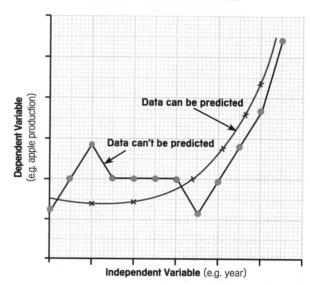

4 **Scattergrams** (scatter diagrams) show the underlying relationship between two variables. This can be made clearer if you include a **line of best fit**. A line of best fit could be a straight line or a smooth curve.

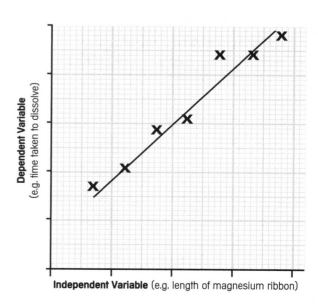

How Science Works Overview

Conclusions **should**…
- describe patterns and relationships between variables
- take all the data into account
- make direct reference to the original hypothesis or prediction
- try to explain the results / observations by making reference to the hypothesis as appropriate.

Conclusions **should not**…
- be influenced by anything other than the data collected (i.e. be biased)
- disregard any data (except anomalous values)
- include any unreasoned speculation.

An **evaluation** looks at the whole investigation. It should consider…
- the original purpose of the investigation
- the appropriateness of the methods and techniques used
- the reliability and validity of the data
- the validity of the conclusions.

The **reliability** of an investigation can be increased by…
- looking at relevant data from secondary sources (i.e. sources created by someone who did not experience first hand or participate in the original experiment)
- using an alternative method to check results
- ensuring results can be reproduced by others.

Science and Society

Scientific understanding can lead to technological developments. These developments can be exploited by different groups of people for different reasons. For example, the successful development of a new drug…
- benefits the drugs company financially
- improves the quality of life for patients
- can benefit society (e.g. if a new drug works, then maybe fewer people will be in hospital, which reduces time off sick, cost to the NHS, etc).

Scientific developments can raise certain **issues**. An issue is an important question that is in dispute and needs to be settled. The resolution of an issue may not be based on scientific evidence alone.

There are several different types of **issue** that can arise:
- **Social** – the impact on the human population of a community, city, country, or the world.
- **Economic** – money and related factors like employment and the distribution of resources.
- **Environmental** – the impact on the planet, its natural ecosystems and resources.
- **Ethical** – what is morally right or wrong; requires a value judgement to be made.

N.B. There is often an overlap between social and economic issues.

Peer Review

Finally, peer review is a process of self-regulation involving qualified professional individuals or experts in a particular field who examine the work undertaken critically. The vast majority of peer review methods are designed to maintain standards and provide credibility for the work that has been undertaken. These methods vary depending on the nature of the work and also on the overall purpose behind the review process.

Evaluating Information

It is important to be able to evaluate information relating to social-scientific issues, for both your GCSE course and to help you make informed decisions in life.

When evaluating information...
- make a list of **pluses** (pros)
- make a list of **minuses** (cons)
- consider how each point might **impact on society**.

You also need to consider whether the source of information is reliable and credible. Some important factors to consider are...
- **opinions**
- **bias**
- **weight of evidence**.

Opinions are personal viewpoints. Opinions backed up by valid and reliable evidence carry far more weight than those based on non-scientific ideas.

Opinions of experts can also carry more weight than non-experts.

Information is **biased** if it favours one particular viewpoint without providing a balanced account.

Biased information might include incomplete evidence or try to influence how you interpret the evidence.

Scientific evidence can be given **undue weight** or dismissed too quickly due to...
- political significance (consequences of the evidence could provoke public or political unrest)
- status of the experiment (e.g. if they do not have academic or professional status, experience, authority or reputation).

Limitations of Science

Although science can help us in lots of ways, it can't supply all the answers. We are still finding out about things and developing our scientific knowledge.

There are some questions that science can't answer. These tend to be questions...
- where beliefs, opinions and ethics are important
- where we don't have enough reproducible, repeatable or valid evidence.

Science can often tell us if something **can** be done, and **how** it can be done, but it can't tell us whether it **should** be done.

Decisions are made by individuals and by society on issues relating to science and technology.

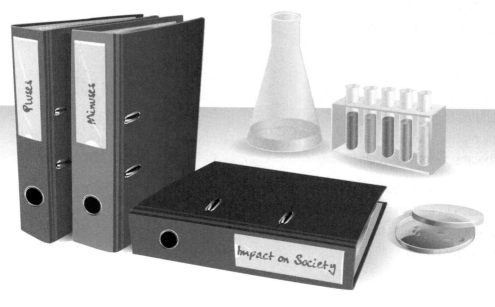

P1 Energy Transfer

Infrared Radiation

Infrared radiation involves the transfer of **heat energy** by electromagnetic radiation, also called **thermal radiation**. No particles of matter are involved in the process.

All objects emit and absorb infrared radiation.

The hotter an object is the more infrared radiation it radiates.

The amount of infrared radiation an object gives out or takes in depends on its **surface**, **shape** and **dimensions**.

An object will emit and absorb infrared radiation faster if there's a bigger difference in temperature between it and its surroundings. Different materials transfer thermal energy at different rates.

At the same temperature dark, matt surfaces...
- emit more infrared radiation than light, shiny surfaces
- absorb more infrared radiation than light, shiny surfaces.

Light, shiny surfaces are good reflectors of infrared radiation. An example of a good reflector is the 'silvering' on the inside of a vacuum flask.

Kinetic Theory

Kinetic theory explains the different **states** and **properties** of **matter** in terms of the movement of the millions and millions of particles (atoms / molecules). The particles of gases, liquids and solids have different amounts of energy.

The atoms / molecules that make up a gas are always moving. **They move very quickly** in **random directions**, colliding with each other and with the walls of the container they are in.

When the temperature increases...
- the gas molecules move faster
- the collisions become more intense.

When the temperature falls...
- the gas molecules move more slowly
- the molecules move closer together
- the collisions become less frequent
- the gas begins to form a liquid.

Eventually the liquid becomes a solid. The atoms / molecules in a solid can only move (**vibrate**) about a **fixed position**, so they form a **regular** and **orderly pattern**.

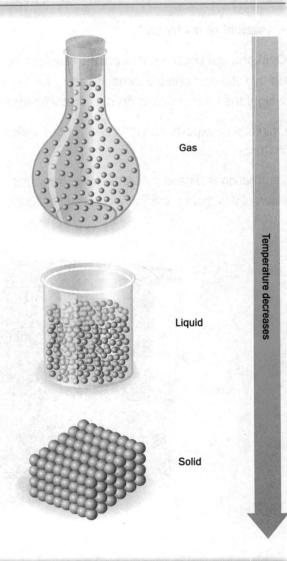

Gas

Liquid

Solid

Temperature decreases

Infrared radiation • Thermal radiation • Kinetic theory

Energy Transfer by Heating

Energy transfer by heating involves the movement of particles. This can be undertaken by a variety of mechanisms including...

- conduction
- convection
- evaporation
- condensation.

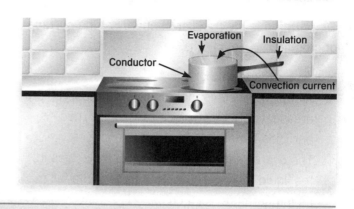

Conduction

Conduction is the transfer of energy by heating without the substance itself moving. For example, metals are good **conductors** of energy:

- As a metal becomes hotter the **atoms vibrate** more vigorously.
- This additional energy is transferred to the cooler parts of the metal by the **free electrons** that roam throughout the metal.

Insulators are materials that have few or no free electrons, so they can't readily transfer their energy by heating.

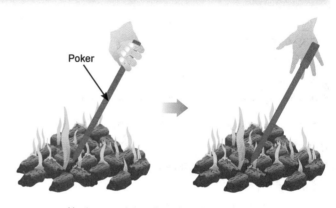

Heat energy is conducted up the poker as the hotter parts transfer energy to the colder parts

Convection

Convection is the transfer of energy by heating through the movement of particles.

Convection occurs in liquids and gases, creating **convection currents**:

1. Particles in the liquid or gas nearest the energy source move **faster**, causing the substance to **expand** and become **less dense**.
2. The warm liquid or gas now rises vertically. As it does so it **cools**, becomes **denser** and eventually sinks.
3. The colder, denser liquid or gas moves into the space created (close to the heat source) and the cycle repeats.

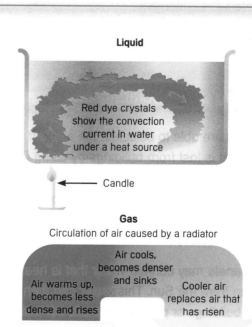

Liquid

Red dye crystals show the convection current in water under a heat source

Candle

Gas
Circulation of air caused by a radiator

Air cools, becomes denser and sinks

Air warms up, becomes less dense and rises

Cooler air replaces air that has risen

Evaporation and Condensation

Evaporation is the transfer of energy at the **surface of a liquid**.

In terms of kinetic theory:

- Atoms / molecules that are moving most rapidly are located at the surface of a liquid. These particles behave like a gas and escape.
- The overall energy of the atoms / molecules in the liquid then reduces. This results in a fall in its temperature, i.e. it cools.

When water evaporates from a surface, it becomes a gas called **water vapour**.

The opposite effect, where the gas or vapour returns to a liquid state at the surface, is called **condensation**. This transfers energy back into the substance at the surface.

Water evaporates quickly when it's hotter. As the water boils, it turns into steam

Rate of Energy Transfer

Under similar conditions different materials will transfer energy by heating at very **different rates**. The rate at which a material transfers energy depends on...

- its **surface area** and **volume**
- the **type** of material it's made from
- the **nature** of the surface with which the material is in contact
- its temperature.

For example...

- cooling fins on a motorbike engine allow the transfer of energy from the engine to the surrounding air a lot faster
- a desert fox has far larger ears than an Arctic fox to allow for a more efficient way of getting rid of unwanted energy.

The **bigger** the **temperature difference** between an object and its surroundings, the **faster** the rate at which energy is transferred.

H

Arc
ene   s:

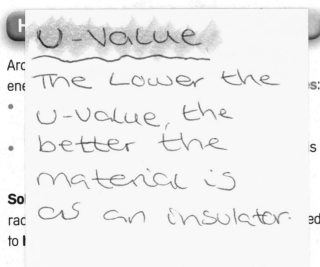

U-Value

The Lower the U-value, the better the material is as an insulator.

So
rad   ed
to

Using Solar Energy / Radiation to Heat Water

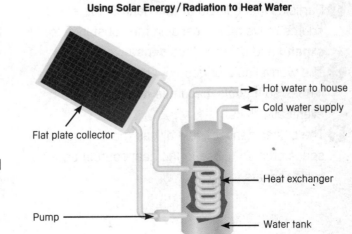

Flat plate collector

Hot water to house
Cold water supply

Heat exchanger

Pump

Water tank

Specific Heat Capacity

Different materials (with identical masses and at the same temperature) can store different amounts of energy.

The quantity known as the **specific heat capacity** is the amount of energy required to change the temperature of 1kg of a material by 1°C.

To work out the energy required use the following equation:

$$E = m \times c \times \theta$$

where E is the energy transferred in joules (J)
m is the mass (kg)
c is the specific heat capacity that has units of J / kg °C
θ is the temperature change (°C)

For example, the specific heat capacity of water is 4200J / kg^{-1} °C

To compare against water, the table below shows the specific heat capacity of various materials.

Material	Specific heat capacity (J / kg°C)
Air	1012
Aluminium	897
Copper	385
Petrol	2220

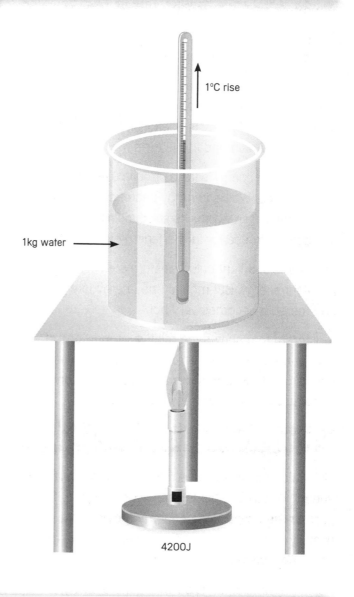

1°C rise

1kg water

4200J

Quick Test

1. What type of radiation do all objects emit?
2. Is the following statement true or false? 'Light, shiny surfaces are good reflectors and poor emitters of infrared radiation.'
3. When a pure solid metal is made, what patterns do the metallic atoms take?
4. What is responsible for metals behaving as good conductors?
5. Give the two main factors that affect the rate of evaporation or condensation.
6. What does the U-value measure?
7. Calculate the energy transferred when 0.1kg of water at 0°C is brought to boiling point (i.e. 100°C). (N.B. the specific heat capacity of water is 4200 J / kg°C.)

Energy Transfers

Energy can be **transferred, usually stored**, or **dissipated**, but it can't be **created** or **destroyed**.

Many devices take in energy in one form and transfer the energy into another form. In doing so only part of the energy is usefully transferred to where it's wanted and in the form that's wanted.

The remaining energy is transferred in a **non-useful way**, i.e. is **wasted**. Wasted energy becomes increasingly spread out and so **warms its surroundings**. In this form it is difficult to use for further energy transfers.

For example, a light bulb transforms electrical energy into light energy. But most of the energy is wasted and the bulb becomes very hot.

A diagram that shows the relative proportions of energy transfers using arrows is called a **Sankey diagram**. The **widths of arrows** are proportional to the **amount of energy** they represent.

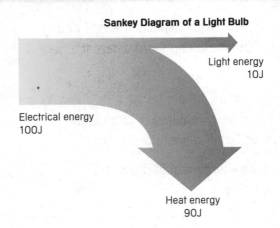

Sankey Diagram of a Light Bulb

Light energy 10J

Electrical energy 100J

Heat energy 90J

Electrical appliances transfer energy for different uses, and some of the energy is wasted:

- A kettle transfers energy in the form of heat (to the water), but energy is also wasted as heat (to the kettle and air) and as sound.
- An electric motor (e.g. drill, washing machine) transfers kinetic energy, but energy is also wasted in the form of heat and sound.

Energy Efficiency

The **efficiency** of a device refers to the proportion of energy (or power) that is usefully transferred. **The greater the proportion** of energy (power) that is usefully transferred, the more efficient and the more **cost-effective** the device is.

Replacing an old television with a more energy efficient one may cost £600, but may also provide an annual saving of £60 per year. The **pay-back time** can be calculated as $\dfrac{£600}{£60 \text{ per year}} = 10$ years

Efficiency values are usually expressed either as a **percentage** or as a **decimal** number. Efficiency can be calculated using the following equation:

$$\text{Efficiency} = \frac{\text{Useful energy or useful power out}}{\text{Total energy or total power in}} \times 100\%$$

For example, only a quarter of the energy supplied to a television is usefully transferred into light and sound. The rest is wasted, so it's only 0.25 or 25% efficient.

Transferring Electrical Energy

Most of the energy transferred to houses and industry is in the form of **electrical energy**.

Electrical energy is easily transferred…
- by heaters to heat surroundings, e.g. a hairdryer
- into light energy, e.g. a lamp
- into sound energy, e.g. stereo speakers
- into kinetic energy (movement), e.g. an electric fan.

The amount of energy transferred by an electrical appliance depends on…
- **how long** the appliance is switched on
- **how fast** (the rate of energy transfer) the appliance transfers energy, i.e. its **power**.

Without a reliable source of electrical energy we could have power cuts – creating the need to use candles for lighting and leaving many people without heating or cooking facilities.

Energy Calculations

Energy is normally measured in **joules** (**J**). **Power** gives a measure of the rate of energy transfer. The power of an appliance is measured in **watts** (W) or sometimes for bigger amounts, **kilowatts** (kW). 1 watt is the same as 1 joule per second (J/s).

To calculate the amount of energy transferred from the mains, the following equation can be used:

$$E = P \times t$$

where E is the energy transferred, P is the power of the appliance and t is the time

In terms of units:
- Energy transferred (in joules) = power (in watts) x time (seconds).
- Energy transferred (in kilowatt-hours) = power (kilowatts) x time (hours).

To calculate the cost of mains electricity or energy transferred by the mains for an appliance, use the following equation:

Total cost (pounds or pence)	=	Number of kilowatt-hours	×	Costs (pounds or pence) per kilowatt-hour

Example

Electricity Statement for the 3rd quarter (3 months).

Present reading	Previous reading	kWh used	Cost per kWh (p)	Charge amount (£)
30803	30332	471	9.45	44.51

kWh calculated by subtracting present reading from previous reading

kWh x cost per kWh
$471 \times \frac{9.45}{100} = £44.51$

Quick Test

1. When energy is transferred part of it may be useful. What happens to the rest?
2. A small wind turbine requires 2000J of energy from the wind but only provides 250J of useful electrical energy. What is the efficiency of the turbine as a percentage?
3. What is a Sankey diagram?
4. What are the units of **a)** electrical energy and **b)** power?
5. The amount of electrical energy transferred by a very bright light bulb is 200 joules per second. What is the power rating of the bulb?
6. A washing machine with a power consumption of 1600W is on for 45 minutes. Calculate **a)** the amount of energy transferred in kWh **b)** the total cost assuming the unit cost is 10p per kilowatt-hour.

P1 Methods We Use to Generate Electricity

Generating Electricity

In some power stations an energy source is used to heat water. The steam produced drives a turbine that is connected to an electrical generator. The different types of energy sources used include…

- **fossil fuels**, e.g. coal, oil and gas, which are burned to heat water or air
- **nuclear fuels**, e.g. uranium and plutonium, in which nuclear fission is used to heat water
- **biofuels**, e.g. wood or methane, which can be burned to heat water.

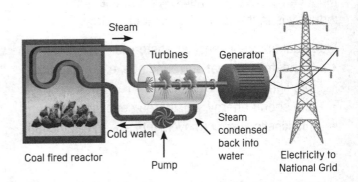

Non-renewable Energy Sources

We depend on **non-renewable energy sources** (e.g. coal, oil, gas and nuclear) for most of our energy needs. They can't be replaced within a lifetime, so they will eventually run out.

Source	Advantages	Disadvantages	Start-up time
Nuclear	• Cost of fuel is low • Rate of fuel use is low • Doesn't produce CO_2 and SO_2 emissions into the atmosphere	• Radioactive waste produced • Difficulty of storing radioactive material for thousands of years • Building new power stations is very costly • Decommissioning is very costly • Accident and radioactive contamination risks are high	Longest
Coal	• Relatively cheap and easy to extract	• Burning coal produces CO_2 (**Greenhouse effect**) and SO_2 (**acid rain**) emissions into the atmosphere • Perhaps only several hundred years of coal left	
Oil	• Has been relatively easy to find • Perhaps large amounts of reserve stocks available	• Burning produces CO_2 and SO_2 emissions into the atmosphere • Significant risk of spillage and pollution • Destruction of wildlife habitats	
Gas	• Has been relatively easy to find • Perhaps large amounts of reserve stocks available • Doesn't produce SO_2 emissions into the atmosphere	• Burning produces CO_2 emissions into the atmosphere (although less than coal or oil) • Expensive pipelines and networks are required • Visual pollution of landscape • Destruction of wildlife habitats	Shortest

Key Words   Fossil fuel • Nuclear fuel • Biofuel • Non-renewable energy source

Renewable Energy Sources

Renewable energy sources will not run out because they are continually being replaced. Most renewable energy sources are caused by the Sun or Moon.

The Sun causes…
* evaporation, which results in rain and flowing water
* convection currents, which result in winds that create waves.

The gravitational pull of the Moon creates tides.

Renewable energy sources can be used directly to drive turbines and generators. New sources include **biofuels**, which can be solid, liquid or gas. Biofuels are obtained from lifeless or living biological material. Biofuels include…
* liquid ethanol (derived from fermented plant material such as sugar cane)
* methane gas (from sludge digesters)
* straw, nutshells and woodchip.

Source	Advantages	Disadvantages
Wind turbines	• No fuel and little maintenance • No polluting gases produced • Can be built offshore	• Land-based turbines give visual and noise pollution • High initial capital building costs • Not very flexible in meeting demand • Variation in wind affects output
Tidal and waves	• No fuel required • No polluting gases produced • Barrage water can be released when demand is high	• Visual pollution and hazard to shipping • Can destroy / alter wildlife habitats • Variations in tides / waves affects output • Very high capital costs to build them
Hydroelectric	• Fast start-up time • No polluting gases produced • Water can be pumped back to the reservoir when demand is low	• Involves damming upland valleys • Destruction of wildlife habitats • Need an adequate rainfall • Very high initial costs
Solar cells	• Uses light from the Sun • Useful in remote locations • No polluting gases emitted • Small-scale production possible	• Depends on light intensity • Use of high cost semiconductor materials • Efficiency is poor • Visual pollution of large areas of solar panels
Biofuels	• Flexible product • Cost effective • Little impact on the environment	• Some pre-processing of the material is required • Limited resources due to land area requirements
Geothermal	• No pollutants produced • Uses naturally occurring hot water and steam directly • Low start-up costs	• Restricted to only certain volcanic areas • Subsidence risk

Often small-scale productions can be set-up and built locally to provide electricity, e.g. solar cells for homes and roadside signs. Although these tend to be uneconomical to connect to, and support, the National Grid, this is now changing following a much larger increase in the number of small-scale productions being used in the UK.

Carbon Capture

A recent and rapidly expanding technology is the capture and storage of carbon dioxide. Capturing CO_2 and reducing its effect in the atmosphere is vitally important in reducing the effects of global warming.

Storing CO_2 in natural containers, such as the old oil and gas fields under the North Sea, is one solution being proposed.

The National Grid

Electricity that is generated in power stations is transferred to homes, schools and industry by the National Grid.

Whilst overhead power lines are visually polluting they are more reliable and relatively easy to maintain compared with power cables underground, which are very costly to install.

Transformers are used to change the potential difference (voltage) of the alternating current (a.c.) supply before and after it is transmitted through the National Grid. Both step-up and step-down transformers are used.

Increasing the potential difference reduces the current required for a given power. This reduction in current reduces the energy losses in the cables when electricity is transferred to consumers.

- **Step-up transformers** increase the potential difference (400 000 volts) allowing power lines to transmit electricity from the power station with reduced energy loss.

- **Step-down transformers** decrease the potential difference (230 volts) and increase the current before it is used by consumers.

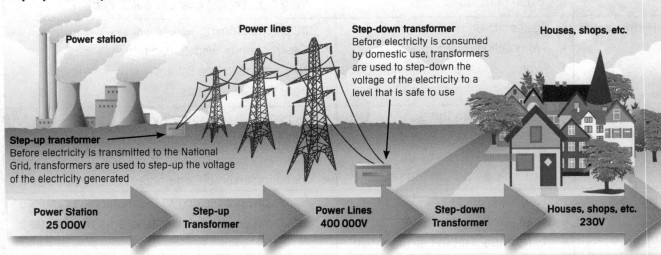

Power station

Power lines

Step-down transformer
Before electricity is consumed by domestic use, transformers are used to step-down the voltage of the electricity to a level that is safe to use

Houses, shops, etc.

Step-up transformer
Before electricity is transmitted to the National Grid, transformers are used to step-up the voltage of the electricity generated

| Power Station 25 000V | Step-up Transformer | Power Lines 400 000V | Step-down Transformer | Houses, shops, etc. 230V |

Quick Test

1. Give two examples of fossil fuels.
2. What is a biofuel?
3. Give one advantage and one disadvantage of solar power.
4. A rapidly evolving technology involves carbon capture. Why is this important and where will it be stored?
5. Why is the potential difference in overhead transmission cables 400 000V?
6. What is the function of a step-down transformer?

Properties of Waves

There are two types of wave:
- A **transverse wave** is where the oscillations are **perpendicular** to the direction of energy transfer, e.g. electromagnetic waves and water waves.
- A **longitudinal wave** is where the oscillations are **parallel** to the direction of energy transfer, e.g. sound waves. These waves show areas of **compression** and **rarefaction**.

All waves transfer energy. **Mechanical waves** (e.g. water waves, waves on springs and shock waves) may be transverse or longitudinal.

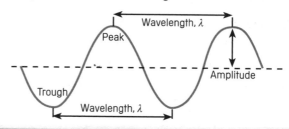

Electromagnetic Spectrum

The electromagnetic spectrum extends from high frequency or high energy (**short wavelength 10^{-15}m**) waves, e.g. gamma rays, to low frequency or low energy (**long wavelength 10^4m**) waves, e.g. **radio waves**.

Visible light is one type of electromagnetic radiation and is the only part of the electromagnetic spectrum that can be seen with the eye. It consists of seven primary bands of colour from **red to violet**.

All waves can be described in terms of their amplitude, frequency and **wavelength**. The **wavelength** is simply the distance between two successive peaks or troughs in a wave.

The connection between frequency and wavelength is given by the **wave equation**:

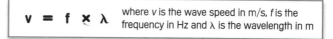

$$v = f \times \lambda$$

where v is the wave speed in m/s, f is the frequency in Hz and λ is the wavelength in m

Waves can be **reflected** and **refracted** when they meet a surface (interface). Transverse and longitudinal waves can also be **diffracted**, for example...
- water waves entering harbours
- radio waves diffracted by hills and large buildings.

When waves are refracted at a surface they undergo a change of direction, except when they are directed at the surface along the **normal**.

Communication

Different parts of the electromagnetic spectrum can be used for communication.

The Electromagnetic Spectrum

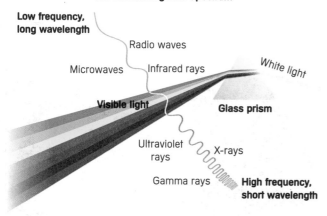

The **amplitude** of an electromagnetic wave is the peak movement of the wave from its rest point. The **frequency** of an electromagnetic wave is the number of waves passing in one second. Frequency is measured in hertz (Hz).

Electromagnetic Waves	Uses
Radio waves	• Television and radio signals allow communication across the Earth
Microwaves	• Mobile phone networks and satellite communication (although there are potential risks of using mobile phones, e.g. possible links with brain tumours) • Cooking – water molecules absorb microwaves and heat up
Infrared	• Remote controls for televisions, etc. • Grills, toasters and radiant heaters (e.g. electric fires) • Optical fibre communication
Visible light	• Morse code with torches, photography, fibre optics

Reflection

When a wave strikes a reflective surface it changes direction. This is called **reflection**.

The **normal line** is a construction line drawn **perpendicular** to the reflecting surface at the point of incidence. The normal line is used to calculate the angles of incidence and reflection.

When an object is viewed in a plane mirror the image formed is…

- **virtual** (i.e. on the opposite side of the mirror)
- **upright** (i.e. in the same orientation)
- **the same size** as the object
- **laterally inverted** (i.e. left becomes right)

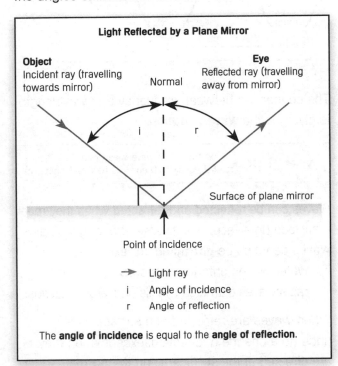

Light Reflected by a Plane Mirror

Object
Incident ray (travelling towards mirror)

Normal

Eye
Reflected ray (travelling away from mirror)

i Angle of incidence

r Angle of reflection

Surface of plane mirror

Point of incidence

→ Light ray
i   Angle of incidence
r   Angle of reflection

The **angle of incidence** is equal to the **angle of reflection**.

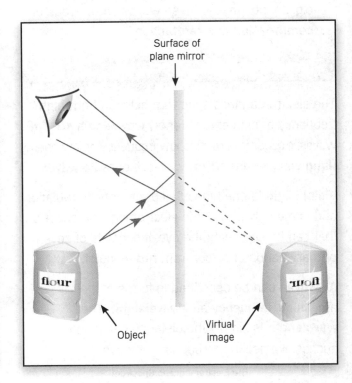

Surface of plane mirror

Object

Virtual image

Sound

Sound also travels as a wave. These are called **longitudinal waves** because they cause vibrations (backwards and forwards) within a material (medium). **Sound waves** can't travel through a vacuum.

The frequency of a **sound wave** is the number of vibrations produced every second, i.e. **hertz** (Hz). Humans can hear sounds in the range between 20Hz and 20 000Hz (20kHz).

The **pitch** of a sound is determined by its **frequency**. As the frequency increases the pitch becomes higher.

Echoes are examples of sound being **reflected** at a **surface**.

Red-shift

If a wave source (e.g. light, sound or microwaves) is moving away from, or towards, an observer, there will be a change in the...

- observed **wavelength**
- observed **frequency**.

The model that's used to describe this phenomenon is known as the Doppler effect. An ambulance racing past you is a good example of the Doppler effect with sound waves.

- When a light source moves **away** from you, the observed **wavelength increases** and the **frequency decreases**. This is known as red-shift.
- When a light source moves **towards** you, the observed **wavelength decreases** and the **frequency increases**. This is known as **blue-shift**.

The Big Bang

The observed red-shift of galaxies supports the idea that...

- the whole Universe is **expanding**
- the expansion began from a very small initial point in a huge explosion known as the **Big Bang**.

Cosmic Microwave Background Radiation (CMBR) is a form of electromagnetic radiation that fills the entire Universe. It comes from radiation that was around shortly after the beginning of the Universe but which has now been stretched.

The Big Bang theory is currently the **only theory** that can explain the existence of CMBR.

The light observed from distant **galaxies** in the Universe is **red-shifted**. In fact the further away a galaxy is, the faster it is moving and the bigger the observed increase in wavelength.

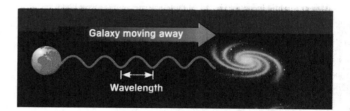

Galaxy moving away
Wavelength

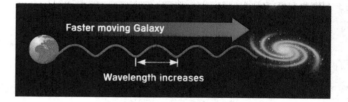

Faster moving Galaxy
Wavelength increases

Quick Test

1. Do radio waves and gamma rays travel through a vacuum (space) at the same speed?
2. What is the amplitude of a wave?
3. When an object is viewed in a plane mirror what does the image look like?
4. What type of wave is a sound wave?
5. Between what two frequencies can humans hear sound?
6. Give two pieces of evidence that the red-shift of light provides in terms of our Universe.

BANG!

1 Different materials require different amounts of energy to raise their temperature by 1°C. In fact the energy (E) required can be calculated using the equation:

$$E = m \times c \times \theta$$

(a) Explain the meanings of the symbols m, c and θ.

....

....

....

.... **(3 marks)**

(b) An electric kettle is used to boil some water.

The amount of water is 0.6kg, and room temperature is taken to be 20°C. If the specific heat capacity of the water is 4200J / kg°C, determine how much energy will be needed to raise the temperature of the water to its boiling point.

....

....

.... **(2 marks)**

(c) The power rating of a kettle is 1.7kW.
(i) Calculate how long it will take for the water to boil (to the nearest minute).

....

.... **(2 marks)**

(ii) What is this time in terms of decimal hours?

....
(1 mark)

(d) Using the information above, determine the amount of energy used in kilowatt-hours.

....

....

.... **(2 marks)**

(e) If the unit cost of electricity is 10p per kilowatt-hour, how much does it cost to boil the water in the kettle?

....

.... **(1 mark)**

2 Different parts of the electromagnetic spectrum are used for communication. For example, visible light is used for photography and Morse code with torches.

(a) From the list below link the type of radiation (**A**, **B** and **C**) with the mode of communication (**1**, **2** and **3**).

A Microwaves   **1** Optical fibre communication

B Radio waves   **2** Mobile phones

C Infrared   **3** TV

(3 marks)

(b) The electromagnetic spectrum is shown below with wavelengths shown in metres. On the spectrum label the positions of microwaves, radio waves and infrared using the letters **A**, **B** and **C** (as above).

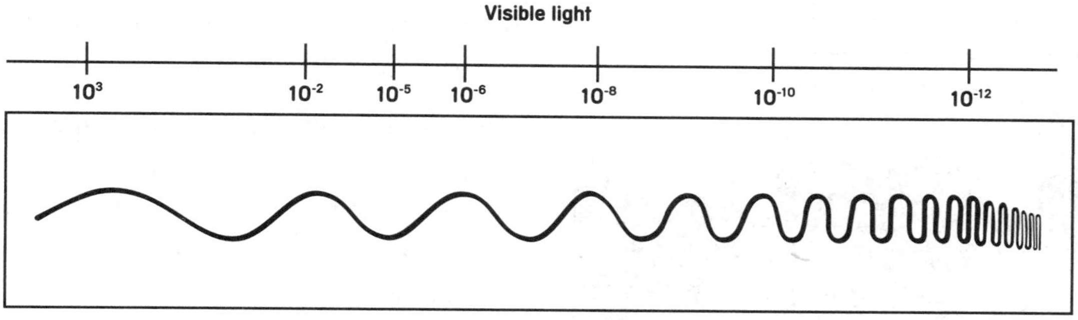

Visible light

| 10^3 | | 10^{-2} | 10^{-5} | 10^{-6} | 10^{-8} | 10^{-10} | 10^{-12} |

(3 marks)

(c) Sound waves are also used in communication. Calculate the wavelength of a sound wave if the speed of sound in air is 330m/s and the frequency is 2000Hz.

(2 marks)

(d) Sound waves travel a lot faster in water than in the air; in fact approximately 1400m/s. Explain why sound waves travel faster in water.

(3 marks)

P2 Forces and their Effects

Resultant Forces

Forces are pushes or pulls. They are measured in units of force called a **newton** (N). Forces may…

- vary in **size**
- act in different **directions**.

Whenever two objects interact, the forces they exert on each other are **equal** and **opposite**. For example, when a stationary object rests on a surface it exerts a **downward force** on the surface due to the attractive force of gravity, which we call its **weight**. The surface it rests on exerts an equal and opposite **upward force**, called a **reaction force**.

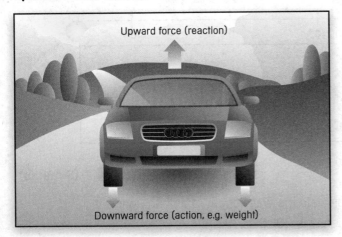

Upward force (reaction)

Downward force (action, e.g. weight)

If a number of different forces act on an object, these forces can be replaced by a single force. This single force has the same effect on the object as the original forces all acting together. This single force is called the **resultant force**.

A resultant force acting on an object may cause a change in its state of rest or motion.

If the resultant force acting on a **stationary** object is…

- zero, the object will remain **stationary**
- not-zero, the object will **accelerate** in the direction of the resultant force.

If the resultant force acting on a **moving** object is…

- zero, the object will continue to move at the **same speed** and in the **same direction**
- not-zero, the body will **accelerate** in the direction of the resultant force.

Forces and Motion

A resultant force acting on an object may cause a change in its state of rest or motion. The change of state of the object will depend on…

- the **size** of the resultant force (the bigger the resultant force the greater the acceleration)
- the **mass** of the object (the bigger the mass the smaller the acceleration).

The relationship between force, mass and acceleration is given by the following formula:

$$F = m \times a \quad \text{OR} \quad a = \frac{F}{m}$$

where F is the resultant force in newtons (N)
m is the mass in kilograms (kg)
a is the acceleration in metres per second squared (m/s²)

This formula says that a force of 1 newton is needed to give a mass of 1kg an acceleration of 1m/s².

For example, a toy car of mass 800g accelerates with a force of 0.4N. Its acceleration is then $\frac{0.4\text{N}}{0.8\text{kg}}$ = 0.5 m/s² (remember, the mass must be in kg).

Speed

The **speed** of an object is just a measure of how fast it is moving. The speed of an object can be worked out if you know...

- the **distance** it travels
- the **time** taken to travel this distance.

You can calculate speed using the following formula:

$$s = \frac{d}{t}$$

where s is the speed in m/s
d is the distance travelled in metres
t is the time taken in seconds

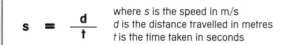

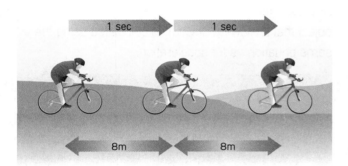

1 sec   1 sec

8m   8m

Speed can also be determined from the **slope** or **gradient** of a **distance–time graph**. The steeper the slope the greater the speed.

The graph shows:

1 A stationary person.

2 A person moving at a constant speed of 2m/s.

3 A person moving at a greater constant speed of 3m/s.

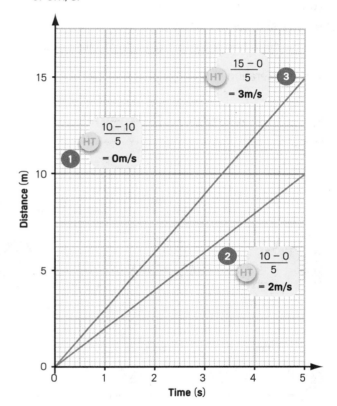

HT $\frac{15 - 0}{5}$ = 3m/s

HT $\frac{10 - 10}{5}$ = 0m/s

HT $\frac{10 - 0}{5}$ = 2m/s

Velocity

The **velocity** of an object and the speed of an object are **not** the same thing. The velocity of an object is its **speed in a certain direction**.

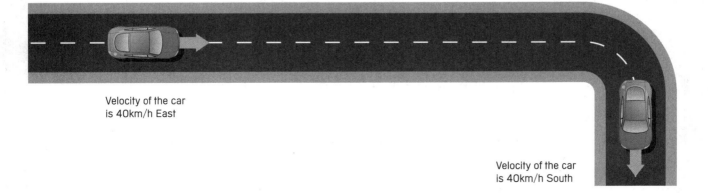

Velocity of the car is 40km/h East

Velocity of the car is 40km/h South

P2 Forces and their Effects

Acceleration

The **acceleration** of an object is the rate at which its **velocity changes**. It is a measure of how quickly an object speeds up or slows down.

To work out the acceleration of any moving object, you need to know…

- the **change in velocity**
- the **time taken** for this change to take place.

The acceleration of an object is given by:

$$\text{Acceleration} = \frac{\text{Change in velocity}}{\text{Time}}$$

The equation is as follows:

$$a = \frac{v - u}{t}$$

where a is the acceleration in m/s^2
v is the final velocity in m/s
u is the initial velocity in m/s
t is the time taken in seconds

The cyclist below increases his velocity by 2m/s every second. So, his acceleration is 2m/s^2.

- His **velocity increases** by the same amount every second.
- The actual **distance** travelled each second **increases**.

Deceleration is a negative acceleration. It describes an object that is slowing down. It is calculated using the same equation as for acceleration.

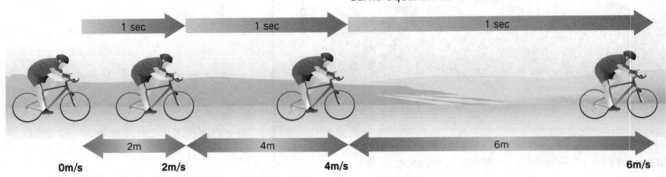

1 sec	1 sec	1 sec
2m	4m	6m
0m/s	2m/s	4m/s	6m/s

Velocity–Time Graphs

The velocity of an object can be represented by a **velocity–time graph**. The slope or gradient of a velocity–time graph gives the **acceleration** of an object.

The steeper the slope, the greater the acceleration.

HT The **area** underneath the line in a velocity–time graph represents the **total distance travelled**.

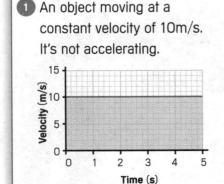

1 An object moving at a constant velocity of 10m/s. It's not accelerating.

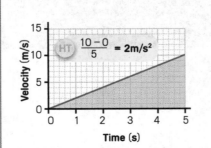

2 An object moving at a constant acceleration of 2m/s^2.

HT $\frac{10 - 0}{5} = 2$m/s^2

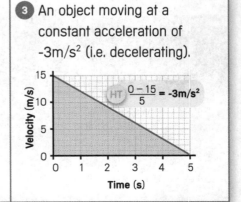

3 An object moving at a constant acceleration of -3m/s^2 (i.e. decelerating).

HT $\frac{0 - 15}{5} = -3$m/s^2

Forces and Braking

Friction is a force that occurs when...
- an object moves through a medium, e.g. air or water
- surfaces slide past each other.

Friction works against the object in the opposite direction to which it is moving, i.e. it's a **resistive force**.

When a vehicle travels at a steady speed the resistive forces (mainly air resistance) balance the **driving force**. The resultant force is the difference between the driving and resistive forces.

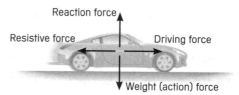

To increase a vehicle's top speed you need either a greater driving force or a reduction in the resistive force, e.g. by altering its shape (become more streamlined).

The **greater the speed** of the vehicle the greater the **braking force needed** to stop it in a certain time or certain distance.

Stopping Distance

The **stopping distance** of a vehicle depends on...
- the **thinking distance** (the distance travelled during the driver's reaction time)
- the **braking distance** (the distance travelled under the braking force).

| Thinking distance | **+** | Braking distance | **=** | Stopping distance |

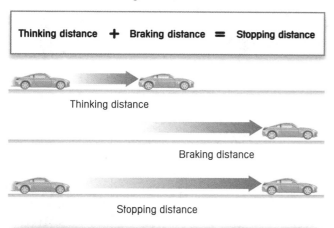

Thinking distance

Braking distance

Stopping distance

The overall stopping distance is increased if...
- the vehicle is travelling at **greater speeds**
- there are **adverse weather conditions**, e.g. wet roads, icy roads, poor visibility, etc
- the **driver is tired** or under the influence of **drugs** or **alcohol** or is **distracted** (e.g. mobile phone) and can't react as quickly as normal
- the **vehicle is in poor condition**, e.g. under-inflated tyres, worn brakes.

Friction forces between the **brakes** and the **wheel**, and between the **wheel** and the **road surface** reduce the kinetic energy of the vehicle. This **kinetic energy** is transformed into heating the brakes resulting in an **increase** in **brake temperature**. If a vehicle's wheels lock when braking, a skid results. Overheating can result in brake failure.

Forces and Weight

All falling objects experience two forces:
- A **downward force**, called **weight** (W).
- An **upward frictional force**, e.g. air resistance or drag through a fluid (R).

Although weight always remains the same, the **faster** an object moves through the air or fluid the **greater** the frictional force that acts on it.

The weight of an object is the force exerted on its mass by **gravity** (sometimes called **gravitational field strength**). Weight is measured in newtons.

To calculate the weight of an object the following equation is used:

$$W = m \times g$$

where the weight W is in newtons
m is the mass in kg and g is the gravitational field strength in newtons per kg (N/kg) (N.B this g has the same units as acceleration, i.e. m/s^2)

P2 Forces and their Effects

Terminal Velocity

An object falling through the air or a fluid will initially accelerate because of the force due to gravity. Eventually the resultant force will be zero as the **weight** and **resistive forces balance**. At this point the object will move at a steady speed, called its **terminal velocity**.

If a skydiver jumps out of an aeroplane, the speed of their descent can be considered in two separate parts:

- **Before** the parachute opens
- **After** the parachute opens.

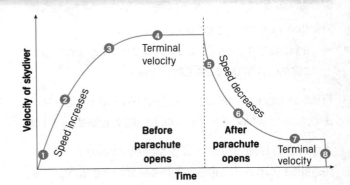

Before the Parachute Opens:

1. The skydiver accelerates due to the force of gravity.
2. The skydiver experiences frictional force due to air resistance in the opposite direction. At this point W is greater than R, so the skydiver continues to accelerate.
3. Speed increases, so does R.
4. R increases until it is the same as W. At this point the **resultant force is zero**. There is no more acceleration and the skydiver falls at a constant speed called the **terminal velocity**.

After the Parachute Opens:

5. The resistive force R is now greatly increased and is far bigger than W.
6. The increase in R decreases the skydiver's speed. As speed is reduced so is the value of R.
7. R decreases until it is the same as W. The forces balance for a second time and the skydiver falls at a steady speed although slower than before. This is a **new terminal velocity**.

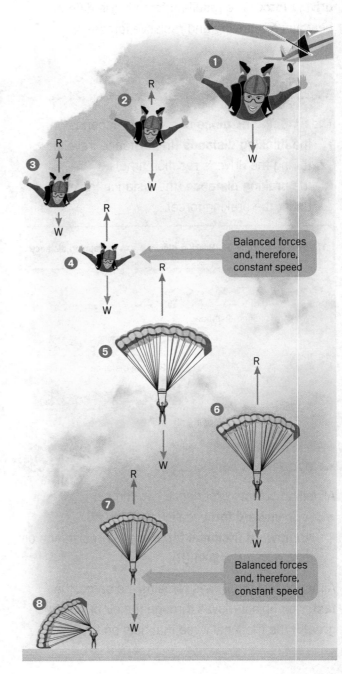

Balanced forces and, therefore, constant speed

Balanced forces and, therefore, constant speed

Forces and Elasticity

A force acting on an object may cause the object to change its shape.

A force applied to an object that's able to recover its original shape when the force is removed is said to be **elastic**, e.g. a spring.

When a force is applied to a spring, work is done in stretching the spring. The energy stored is called **elastic potential energy**. When the force is removed, the energy stored is used to bring the object back to its original shape.

For elastic objects, like springs, the extension is directly proportional to the force applied, provided that the limit of proportionality is not exceeded. The equation for this is as follows:

$$F = k \times e$$

where *F* is the applied force in newtons
e is the extension in metres
k is the proportionality constant, called the **spring constant**, measured in units of N/m

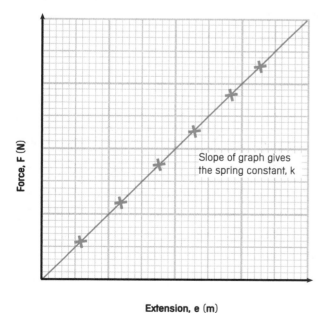

Slope of graph gives the spring constant, k

Force, F (N)

Extension, e (m)

Beyond the elastic limit the object permanently deforms.

Key Words   Elastic • Elastic potential energy • Spring constant

P2 The Kinetic Energy of Objects

Forces and Energy

When a force causes an object to move through a distance, work is done on the object and energy is transferred. Both **work done** (W) and energy transferred (E) are measured in joules (J).

The amount of work done, force and distance are related by the equation:

$$W = F \times d$$

where W is the work done in joules, F is the force applied in newtons and d is the distance moved in the direction of the force in metres

Work done against frictional force mainly transfers energy to the surroundings and heats them.

Power is the work done in a given time and is given by the equation:

$$P = \frac{E}{t}$$

where P is the power in watts, E is the energy transferred in joules and t is the time taken in seconds

Gravitational Potential Energy

Gravitational potential energy is the energy that an object has due to its vertical position in the gravitational field. Work is done against the gravitational force and the object gains gravitational potential energy resulting from an increase in its height.

Gravitational potential energy can be calculated using the equation:

$$E_p = m \times g \times h$$

where E_p is the change in gravitational potential energy (joules), m is the mass in kilograms, g is the gravitational field strength in N/kg (approx. 10 on Earth), and h is the change in height in metres

Kinetic Energy and Momentum

The **kinetic energy** of an object is the energy it has due to its motion. Kinetic energy depends on…
- the **mass** of the object
- the **speed** of the object.

Kinetic energy can be calculated using the equation:

$$E_k = \frac{1}{2} \times m \times v^2$$

where E_k is the kinetic energy in joules, m is the mass in kilograms and v is the speed in m/s

A moving car has kinetic energy because it has both mass and speed. If it moves at greater speed it has more kinetic energy despite the mass being the same. A lorry moving at the same speed as a car will have greater kinetic energy due to its much greater mass.

During collisions the kinetic energy can be dissipated by using energy-absorbing devices such as air bags, crumple zones, seat belts and side impact bars in cars.

Unlike friction brakes, regenerative braking transfers unused energy back into useful electrical energy to recharge batteries and increase the overall efficiency of a vehicle, e.g. in hybrid cars and electric trains.

Momentum is a fundamental property of moving objects. It depends on…
- the **mass** of the object
- the **velocity** of the object.

Momentum can be calculated using the formula:

$$p = m \times v$$

where p is the momentum in kilograms metre per second (kg m/s), m is the mass in kilograms and v is the velocity in m/s

A moving car has momentum as it has both mass and velocity (speed in a certain direction). If the car moves with greater velocity, then it has more momentum providing its mass is the same.

For example, a car of mass 1200kg is moving with a velocity of 20m/s. Its momentum is 1200kg x 20m/s = 24000kg m/s. If the car moves with a new velocity of 30m/s then its new momentum is 1200kg x 30m/s = 36000kg m/s.

Conservation of Momentum

Momentum (like velocity) has…

- **size** (magnitude)
- **direction**.

The direction of movement is important when undertaking calculations involving momentum.

For example:

- Car A of mass 1400kg (moving from left to right) has a velocity of 20m/s to the right and, consequently, a momentum of 28000kg m/s to the right.
- Car B of mass 1400kg (moving from right to left) has a velocity of 20m/s to the left, i.e. -20m/s and momentum of 28000kg m/s to the left or -28000kg m/s with respect to car A because it is moving in the opposite direction to car A. Its momentum is -28000kg m/s.

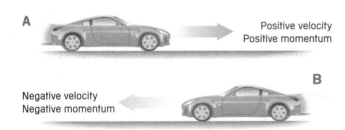

A fundamental principle of momentum is that in a closed system, i.e. where no other external forces act, the total momentum before an event is equal to the total momentum **after the event**. This is called the **conservation of momentum**.

Example

Two cars are travelling in the same direction along a road. Car A collides with the back of car B and they stick together. Calculate their velocity after the collision.

Before

After

Car A + Car B mass 2200kg

Momentum before collision:

= Momentum of A + Momentum of B
= (mass x velocity of A) + (mass x velocity of B)
= (1200kg x 20m/s) + (1000kg x 9m/s)
= 24 000kg m/s + 9000kg m/s
= 33 000kg m/s

Momentum after collision:

= Momentum of A and B
= (mass of A + mass of B) x (velocity of A + B)
= (1200 + 1000) x v
= 2200v

Since momentum is conserved:

Total momentum before = Total momentum after

$$33\,000 = 2200v$$

$$\text{So, } v = \frac{33\,000}{2200}$$

$$= \textbf{15m/s}$$

Quick Test

1. What is 'work done' in terms of energy?
2. What is the name given to the amount of work done per second?
3. Calculate the kinetic energy of a car of mass 1000kg moving at 12m/s.
4. What is meant by the phrase 'conservation of momentum'?

P2 Currents in Electrical Circuits

Static Electricity

Some insulating materials can become electrically charged when they are rubbed against each other. Unless it is **discharged**, the electrical charge, called **static electricity**, stays on the material.

Static electricity builds up when electrons (negative charge) are 'rubbed off' one material on to another. The material…

- **gaining** electrons becomes **negatively** charged
- **losing** electrons becomes **positively** charged.

For example, a Perspex rod rubbed with a cloth becomes positively charged and an ebonite rod rubbed with fur becomes negatively charged.

Perspex Rod Rubbed with Cloth

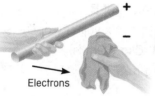

Ebonite Rod Rubbed with Fur

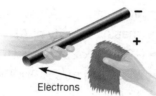

When two electrically charged objects are brought together they exert a force on each other. They are either attracted or repelled:

- Materials with the **same** charge **repel** each other, e.g. Perspex and Perspex.
- Materials with **different** charges **attract** each other, e.g. Perspex and ebonite.

Perspex Rod repels a Perspex Rod

Perspex Rod attracts an Ebonite Rod

Although static is transferred between the surfaces of materials, electrical charges can also readily move through some materials, e.g. metals. This is because there are electrons from their atoms that are free to move through the metal structure (called **free electrons**).

Current

An electric **current** through a circuit is a **flow of electric charge**. The **size** of the electric current is the **rate of flow** of electric charge and is given by the following equation:

$$I = \frac{Q}{t}$$

where *I* is the current in amperes (amps, A), *Q* is the charge in coulombs (C) and *t* is the time in seconds (s)

Potential Difference

An electric current will flow through an electrical component (or device) if there is a **potential difference** (**voltage**) across the ends of the component. The potential difference between two points in an electric circuit is the work done (energy transferred) per coulomb of charge that passes between the points.

Potential difference is given by the equation:

$$V = \frac{W}{Q}$$

where *V* is the potential difference in volts (V), *W* is the work done in joules (J) and *Q* is the charge in coulombs (C)

Static electricity • Current • Potential difference (voltage)

Resistance

The amount of current that flows through a component depends on...

- the **potential difference** across the component
- the **resistance** of the component.

All components resist the flow of current through them. Resistance is a measure of how hard it is to get a current through a component at a particular potential difference. Resistance is measured in **ohms**, which have the symbol Ω.

The greater the resistance of the components...

- the **smaller** the **current** that flows for a particular potential difference

OR

- the **greater** the **potential difference** needed to maintain a particular current.

To calculate the current, potential difference or resistance the following equation is used:

$$V = I \times R$$

where *V* is the potential difference in volts (V), *I* is the current in amperes (amps A), and *R* is the resistance in ohms (Ω)

Circuits

In a circuit...

- the potential difference (p.d) provided by cells connected in series is the sum of the potential difference of each cell
- the potential difference is measured in volts (V) using a **voltmeter** connected in **parallel**
- the current is measured in amperes (A) using an **ammeter** connected in **series**.

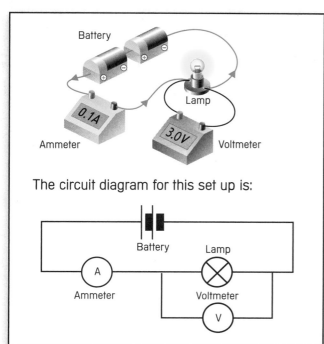

The circuit diagram for this set up is:

Standard symbols are used to represent the various components in circuit diagrams. For example:

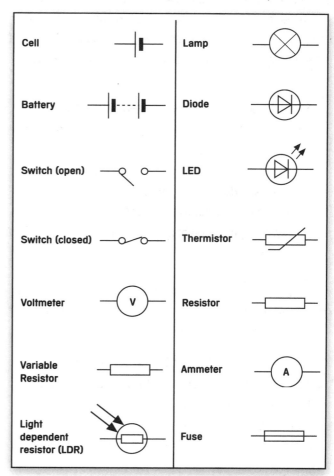

Current–Potential Difference Graphs

Current–potential difference graphs show how the current through a component varies with the potential difference across it.

The resistance of a **light dependent resistor** (**LDR**) depends on the amount of light falling on it. Its **resistance decreases** as the amount of **light** falling on it **increases**. This allows more current to flow.	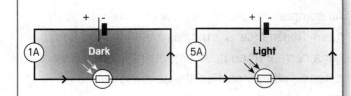
The resistance of a **thermistor** depends on its **temperature**. Its **resistance decreases** as the **temperature** of the thermistor **increases**. This allows more current to flow.	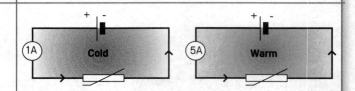
As long as the temperature of the **resistor** stays constant, the current through the resistor is directly proportional to the potential difference across the resistor. This is regardless of which direction the current is flowing, i.e. if one doubles, the other also doubles.	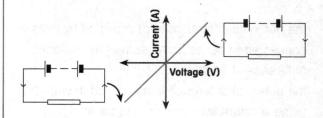
As the temperature of the **filament lamp** increases, and the bulb gets brighter, then the resistance of the lamp increases. (HT) This is due to the greater vibrations of the metallic ions in the filament wire gradually preventing the flow of free electrons.	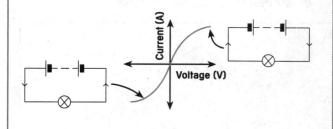
A **diode** allows a current to flow through it in **one direction only**. It has a very high resistance in the reverse direction so no current flows. A light emitting diode (LED) emits light when a current flows through it in the forward direction. There is an increasing use of LEDs for lighting as they use a much smaller current than other forms of lighting and are most cost-effective.	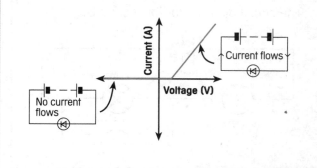

Series Circuits

For components connected **in series**:

- The total resistance (R) is the sum of the resistance of each component, $R = R_1 + R_2$
- There is the same current through each component, $I = I_1 = I_2$
- The total potential difference of the supply (V) from the battery is shared between the components, $V = V_1 + V_2$

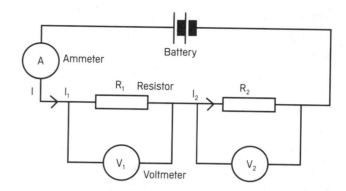

Parallel Circuits

For components connected **in parallel**:

- The potential difference across each component is the same, $V = V_1 = V_2$
- The total current through the whole circuit is the sum of the currents through the separate components, $I = I_1 + I_2$

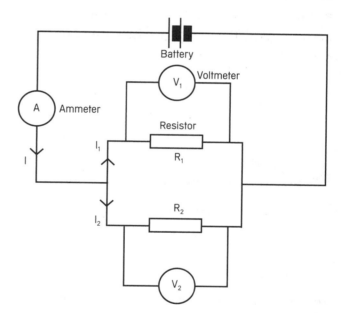

Quick Test

1. What will two materials with the same charge do if they are brought together?
2. What name is given to the rate of flow of electric charge?
3. What unit is used for resistance?
4. If identical components are connected in parallel, what is the current through each component?
5. What happens to the resistance of a thermistor when its temperature increases?

P2 Mains Electricity

Direct and Alternating Currents

Wet cell, dry-cell non-rechargeable, and dry-cell rechargeable batteries supply a current that always passes in the same direction. This is called **direct current (d.c)**. The trace for d.c. on a cathode ray oscilloscope is a straight line.

Alternating current (a.c.) is one that is constantly changing direction (oscillates). The trace for a.c. on a cathode ray oscilloscope is a wave. The **period** and **amplitude** of the wave form determines the nature of the a.c. supply.

Mains electricity is an a.c. supply. In the UK it has a frequency of 50 cycles per second (50 hertz) and is about 230V. The voltage, if it isn't used safely, can kill.

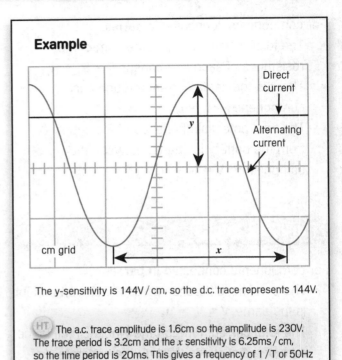

Example

The y-sensitivity is 144V/cm, so the d.c. trace represents 144V.

HT The a.c. trace amplitude is 1.6cm so the amplitude is 230V. The trace period is 3.2cm and the *x* sensitivity is 6.25ms/cm, so the time period is 20ms. This gives a frequency of 1/T or 50Hz

The Three-pin Plug

Most electrical devices are connected to the mains electricity supply using a **cable** and a **three-pin plug**. The plug is inserted into a socket on the ring main circuit.

The materials used for the plug and cable are designed to reduce risk of electrocution. The following are the main properties of the cable and plug:

- The **inner cores** of the wires are made of copper because it's an excellent conductor.
- The **outer layers** of the wires are made from flexible **plastic** because it's a **good insulator**.
- Wires comprise of either **two-core** or **three-core** cable. The three-core carries an earth wire.
- The **pins** of the plug are made from **brass** because it's a **good conductor**, strong and stiff.
- The casing is made from plastic or rubber because both are good insulators.

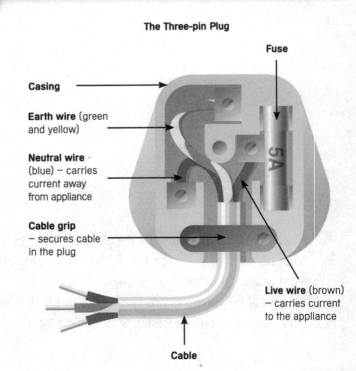

The Three-pin Plug

Fuse

Casing

Earth wire (green and yellow)

Neutral wire (blue) – carries current away from appliance

Cable grip – secures cable in the plug

Live wire (brown) – carries current to the appliance

Cable

5A

Direct current (d.c.) • Alternating current (a.c.)

Circuit Breakers and Fuses

If an electrical fault occurs there is an increase in the current flow. A **fuse** or **circuit breaker** in the circuit provides a disconnection in the live wire, effectively switching off the circuit.

Depending on the type of electrical appliance, the plug will be fitted with fuses that have **different ratings**, e.g. 3A, 5A, 13A. When the current in the **fuse** wire exceeds the rating of the fuse it will **melt**, **breaking the circuit**.

The thicker the cable, the **higher** the rating of the **fuse value**. Fuses have to be replaced each time the circuit is overloaded.

Some modern circuits are protected by using circuit breakers, which **automatically** break an electric circuit if it becomes overloaded. Circuit breakers are easily **reset** by pressing a button.

Some circuits are protected by **Residual Current Circuit Breakers** (**RCCBs**). These operate by detecting a **difference** in the current between the **live** and **neutral** wires. These devices operate much faster than a fuse.

Earthing

Devices that have outer **metal cases** are usually **earthed**. The outer case of an electrical appliance is connected to the earth pin in the plug through the earth wire.

The earth wire and fuse work together to protect the appliance (and the user).

If a fault occurs:

1. The case will become live.
2. The current will then 'flow to earth' through the earth wire as this offers least resistance.
3. This overload of current will cause the fuse to melt (or circuit breaker to trip), breaking the circuit.
4. The appliance (and user) are therefore protected.

Some appliances, e.g. drills, are **double insulated**, and therefore have no earth wire connection.

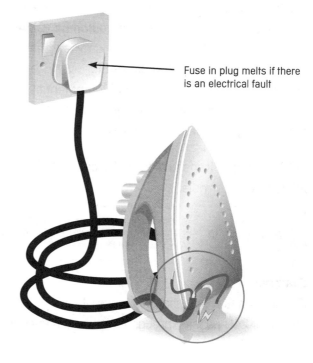

Fuse in plug melts if there is an electrical fault

Energy Transfer

When an electrical **charge** (current) flows through a **resistor** (e.g. electrical device or appliance), the resistor gets **hot**. Some of the electrical energy is used but a lot of energy is wasted, which usually heats the surroundings.

In a filament bulb only 5% of the energy goes into light, the remaining 95% is wasted as heat energy. Less energy is wasted in power-saving lamps such as **Compact Fluorescent Lamps** (CFLs).

Power

The rate at which energy is transferred by an appliance is called the **power**.

Power can be calculated using the following formula:

$$P = \frac{E}{t}$$

where *P* is the power in watts (W)
E is the energy transferred in joules (J)
t is the time in seconds (s)

A much more useful expression for power is one that connects power with the current and potential difference:

$$P = I \times V$$

where *P* is the power in watts (W)
I is the current in amperes (amps, A)
V is the potential difference in volts (V)

For example, a vacuum cleaner rated at 1100W and using mains electricity (230V), provides a current of $\frac{P}{V} = \frac{1100W}{230V} = 4.8A$. A fuse with a rating of 5A would be suitable for the safe operation of this appliance.

Important factors to consider when buying household appliances (e.g. fridges, washing machines and dishwashers) are their energy efficiency and their power rating. Equally important is their ease of maintenance and location, which helps reduce heat loss and maintain efficiency.

Charge

The amount of electrical **charge** that passes any point in a circuit is measured in **coulombs** (C). As charge passes through a device energy is transferred. The amount of energy transferred for every coulomb of charge depends on the size of the potential difference. The **greater** the potential difference, the **more** energy is transferred per coulomb.

(HT) The energy transferred can be calculated using the following formula:

$$E = V \times Q$$

where *E* is energy in joules (J), *V* is the potential difference in volts (V) and *Q* is the charge in coulombs (C)

Example

If a circuit has a potential difference of 1.5V, and a charge of 24C passes through it, how much energy is transferred?

Energy transferred = p.d. x Charge
= 1.5V x 24C
= **36 joules**

Remember, the charge gained this energy from the battery. It was transferred to the bulb whilst the circuit was switched on

Quick Test

1. Name two devices that give protection when an electrical fault occurs.
2. What colour is the earth wire in a three-pin plug?
3. A washing machine has a power rating of 2300W and uses mains electricity. What is the size of fuse that must be used in the three-pin plug?
4. A filament lamp transfers 690 joules of energy using mains electricity. What is the amount of charge that passes through the circuit?

Atoms

Atoms are the basic particles from which all matter is made. The basic structure of an **atom** is an extremely tiny central nucleus composed of **protons** (positive charge) and **neutrons** (no electrical charge) surrounded by **electrons** (negative charge).

This model of the atom, the nuclear model, was based on results from the Rutherford and Marsden scattering experiments and replaced the earlier 'plum pudding model'.

A Fluorine Atom

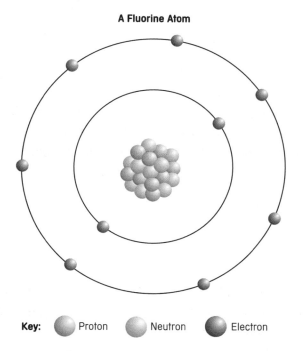

Key: ⚪ Proton ⚪ Neutron ⚫ Electron

In an atom the number of **electrons** is equal to the number of **protons** in the nucleus. So the atom as a whole has no electrical charge and is therefore electrically **neutral**. In the nuclear model most of the atom is empty space.

Atoms of different elements have different numbers of protons (and electrons).

The number of protons in an atom therefore defines the element.
- The number of **protons** in an atom is called its **atomic number**.
- The number of **protons and neutrons** in an atom is called its **mass number**.

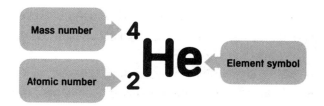

Atomic Particle	Relative Mass	Relative Charge
Proton	1	+1
Neutron	1	0
Electron	$\frac{1}{2000}$	-1

The size of the nucleus is about 10^5 times smaller than the size of the atom.

Isotopes and Ions

Some atoms of the **same element** can have different numbers of **neutrons**. These are called **isotopes**.

For example, oxygen has three common isotopes, $^{16}_{8}O$, $^{17}_{8}O$ and $^{18}_{8}O$ with only $^{16}_{8}O$ being stable.

Atoms may also lose or gain electrons to form charged particles called **ions**. An atom that has gained electrons is called a **negative ion**. An atom that has lost electrons is a **positive ion**. Positively charged ions attract negatively charged ions and can form a strong bond, e.g. sodium chloride (salt).

P2 The Decay of Radioactive Substances

Unstable Nuclei

Isotopes of atoms that have too many or too few neutrons form **unstable nuclei**. The nuclei may disintegrate by **randomly emitting radiation**. Atoms of these isotopes are radioactive (also called **radioactive** isotopes, radioisotopes or radionuclides). The process of disintegration is called **radioactive decay**.

Radioactive decay is all around us and is commonly referred to as **background radiation**. Background radiation is **not harmful** to our health as it occurs in very small amounts or radiation doses. Actual levels depend on where you live and what occupation you do.

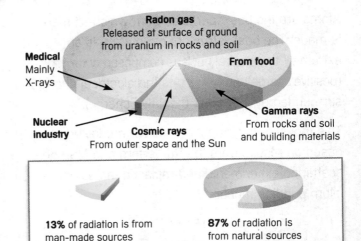

Radon gas
Released at surface of ground from uranium in rocks and soil

Medical Mainly X-rays

From food

Nuclear industry

Cosmic rays From outer space and the Sun

Gamma rays From rocks and soil and building materials

13% of radiation is from man-made sources

87% of radiation is from natural sources

Radioactive Decay

The radioactive decay process can result in the formation of a different atom with a different number of protons.

Three examples of this are...

- **alpha radiation (α)**
- **beta radiation (β)**
- **gamma (γ) radiation**.

Unlike alpha and beta decay, gamma emissions have no effect on the internal structure of the nucleus. Gamma radiation is a form of electromagnetic radiation that carries away any surplus energy from the nucleus.

Gamma radiation can be used for example in radiotherapy to kill cancer cells and shrink malignant tumours.

Radiation can cause damage to living cells. Inside the body alpha radiation is most dangerous as it is easily absorbed by cells whereas beta and gamma radiation are less harmful as they easily pass though the cells. Outside the body the roles are reversed with alpha radiation less harmful and beta and gamma considerably more dangerous.

Alpha Decay

In alpha decay the original atom decays by ejecting an **alpha particle** from its nucleus.

An alpha particle is a huge particle. It's identical to a **helium nucleus**, consisting of **two protons** and **two neutrons**, and symbolised by ^4_2He. In alpha decay a completely new atom is formed.

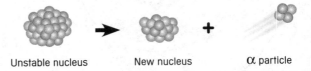

Unstable nucleus   New nucleus   α particle

(HT) For example, Radium-226 decays by alpha emission to form Radon-222, a radioactive gas. The nuclear equation for this decay process is:

$$^{226}_{88}\text{Ra} \longrightarrow {}^{222}_{86}\text{Rn} + {}^4_2\text{He}$$

Beta Decay

In beta decay the original atom decays by changing a **neutron** into a **proton** and an **electron**.

The newly formed high-energy electron is ejected from the nucleus. To distinguish it from orbiting electrons around an atom, the electron emitted is called a **beta particle** with the symbol β.

Unstable nucleus   New nucleus   β particle

Key Words   Unstable nuclei • Radioactive • Background radiation • Gamma radiation • Alpha particle • Beta particle

Beta Decay (Cont.)

(HT) For example, Radon-222 also decays by alpha emission to give Polonium-218. This new atom is also radioactive and decays by beta emission to give Astatine-218. The nuclear equation for this decay is:

$$^{218}_{84}\text{Po} \longrightarrow {}^{218}_{85}\text{At} + {}^{0}_{-1}\beta$$

Notice how the top and bottom numbers balance on either side of the equation. The beta particle carries a negative charge.

Beta decay is used in medical imaging (PET scans) as tracers to highlight and diagnose cancers.

Ionisation and Penetration Power

When radiation collides with **neutral** atoms or molecules in a substance, the atoms or molecules may become charged due to electrons (the outer electrons surrounding the atoms or molecules) being 'knocked out' of the orbiting structure during the collision.

This alters their structure, leaving the atoms or molecules as **ions** (i.e. atoms with an electrical charge) or as **charged particles**.

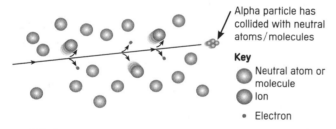

Alpha particle has collided with neutral atoms/molecules

Key
- Neutral atom or molecule
- Ion
- Electron

Each type of emitted radiation (alpha, beta, gamma) has a different...

- degree of **ionising power**
- ability to **penetrate** materials
- **range** in air
- amount of **deflection** in electric and magnetic fields.

(HT) The degree of deflection depends on...

- the **relative masses** of the alpha particle compared to the beta particle
- the **charge** on each particle (+2 for alpha particle and -1 for the beta particle).

Particle	Description	Ionising Power	Penetration	Affected by Electric and Magnetic Fields
Alpha (α)	• Helium nucleus • Positive particle	Strong	Stopped by paper or skin or 6cm of air	Yes, but opposite to beta particles
Beta (β)	• Negative electron	Weak	Stopped by 3mm of aluminium	Yes, bent strongly, but opposite to alpha particles
Gamma (γ)	• Electromagnetic radiation • Very short wavelength	Very weak	Reduced but not stopped by lead	No

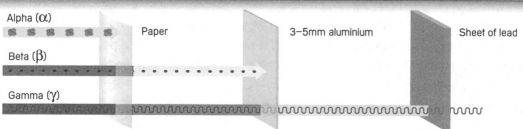

Alpha (α)   Paper   3–5mm aluminium   Sheet of lead

Beta (β)

Gamma (γ)

Half-life

The **half-life** of a radioactive isotope is a measurement of the time it takes for the rate of decay (count-rate) to halve **or** the time required for half of the original population of radioactive atoms to decay.

A radioactive isotope that has a very long half-life remains active for a very long time.

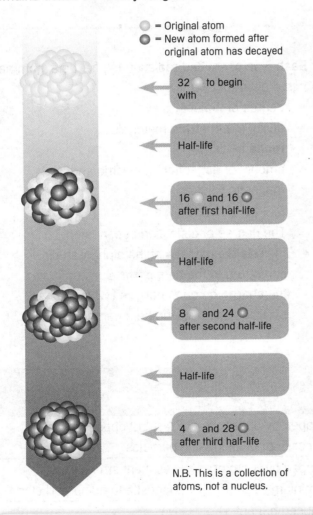

○ = Original atom
● = New atom formed after original atom has decayed

32 ○ to begin with

Half-life

16 ○ and 16 ● after first half-life

Half-life

8 ○ and 24 ● after second half-life

Half-life

4 ○ and 28 ● after third half-life

N.B. This is a collection of atoms, not a nucleus.

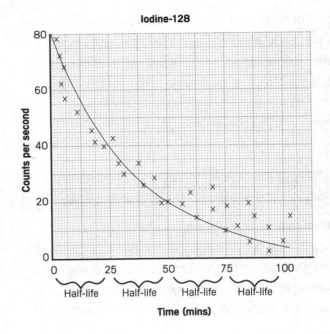

Iodine-128

The graph shows the count rate (using a Geiger counter) from a sample of radioactive Iodine-128 against time. It shows that...

- the initial count rate was 80 counts per second
- after 25 minutes (1 half-life) the count rate has fallen to 40 counts per second
- after two half-lives the count rate is only 20 counts per second.

Radioactive isotopes can have half-lives between fractions of a second to tens of thousands of years.

The choice of which radioisotope to use depends on its purpose and whether it is used internally or externally to diagnose or to treat.

Quick Test

1. An element, E, is represented in the following way: $^M_A E$. What do the letters M and A stand for?
2. Radioactive nuclei can decay by emitting alpha particles. What is an alpha particle?
3. In a magnetic field alpha particles, beta particles and gamma radiation behave differently. Which particle is not deflected at all? Give your reasons.
4. What is meant by the term 'half-life' of a radioactive isotope?

Nuclear Fission

Nuclear fission is the **splitting** of an atomic nucleus. It's used in nuclear reactors to release **energy** to make electricity.

The two fissionable substances in common use in nuclear reactors are **uranium-235** and **plutonium-239**.

For fission to occur the urananium-235 or plutonium-239 nucleus must first **absorb** a neutron. The nucleus then becomes unstable and splits into two smaller nuclei, releasing two or three more neutrons and a lot of energy.

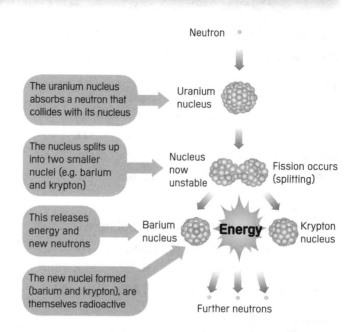

Neutron

The uranium nucleus absorbs a neutron that collides with its nucleus → Uranium nucleus

The nucleus splits up into two smaller nuclei (e.g. barium and krypton) → Nucleus now unstable — Fission occurs (splitting)

This releases energy and new neutrons → Barium nucleus — **Energy** — Krypton nucleus

The new nuclei formed (barium and krypton), are themselves radioactive

Further neutrons

Chain Reaction

The neutrons released in fission may themselves go on to collide with other uranium-235 or plutonium-239 nuclei, producing further neutrons and energy in a process called a **chain reaction**. Nuclear reactors control the rate of this chain reaction to release the energy required.

The new neutrons produced by nuclear fission can each cause a new fission. This is a **chain reaction**. It carries on and on and on

Energy

Energy   **Energy**   **Energy**

The energy is released and heats the surroundings. Each fission reaction only releases a tiny amount of energy, but there are billions and billions of reactions every second

P2 Nuclear Fission and Nuclear Fusion

Nuclear Fusion

Nuclear fusion is the **joining** together of two or more atomic nuclei to form a larger atomic nucleus.

To achieve nuclear fusion a lot of energy is required.

A nuclear fusion reaction (when started) will release more energy than it uses. This makes it **self-sustaining**, i.e. some of the energy produced is used to drive further fusion reactions.

An example is the fusion of two isotopes of hydrogen, called **deuterium** and **tritium**. When they are forced together under high pressure, the deuterium and tritium nuclei fuse together to form a **helium atom** and a **neutron** and a lot of energy.

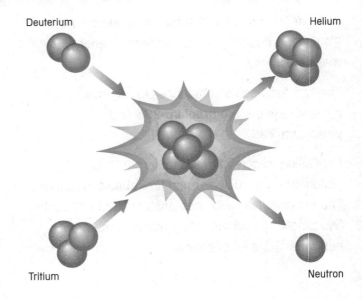

Deuterium — Helium — Tritium — Neutron

Star Formation

Nuclear fusion is the process by which energy is released in stars. In the core of our nearest star, the Sun, hydrogen is being continuously converted into helium through nuclear fusion. This process provides the energy to keep the Sun hot and to allow life on Earth.

Stars, like our Sun, form when enough dust and gas from space are pulled together by gravitational forces, which always attract each other. This forms a **nebula** where a **protostar** is then formed.

Forcing material together increases the temperature and density, and nuclear fusion reactions start releasing huge amounts of energy. Eventually the attractive **gravitational forces** balance with the **repulsive forces** produced by radiation to make a star **stable**.

The newly formed star becomes a **main sequence** star. It will remain like this for many millions or billions of years until its supply of hydrogen runs out.

During the formation process smaller masses within the protostar may be attracted by the dominant larger mass to become **planets**.

Star Formation

During its time on the main sequence, a star will produce all of the naturally occurring elements through the fusion process up to iron.

Key Words   **Nuclear fusion • Nebula • Protostar • Main sequence**

Stellar Evolution

Eventually the hydrogen within a star runs out. What happens next is determined by the size (mass) of the star.

Stars about the Size of the Sun

1. Star leaves the main sequence and becomes a **red giant**.
2. It continues to cool before collapsing under its own gravity to become a **white dwarf**.
3. It continues to cool and loses its brightness to become a **black dwarf**.

Stars Much Bigger than the Sun

1. Star leaves the main sequence and become a **red super giant**.
2. It cools but shrinks very rapidly and explodes as a **supernova**. This explosion releases massive amounts of energy, dust and gas into space, and forms elements heavier than iron.
3. Depending on the precise mass of the remnants either a **neutron star** or a **black hole** is formed.
4. The dust and gas form new stars.

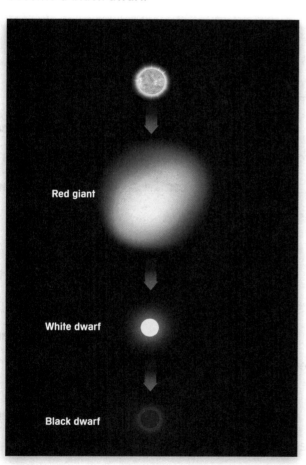

Red giant

White dwarf

Black dwarf

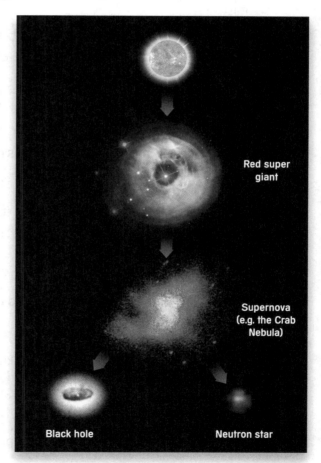

Red super giant

Supernova (e.g. the Crab Nebula)

Black hole

Neutron star

Quick Test

1. Give an example of a fissionable material used in nuclear power stations.
2. What is meant by the term 'chain reaction'?
3. Where is nuclear fusion the dominant energy releasing process?
4. What is the heaviest element that can be produced in Sun-type stars by nuclear fusion?

1 **a)** The diagram shows the position of the Sun in the main sequence of events when the Sun's energy begins to run out. The size of the circles provide an indication as to the size of star involved.

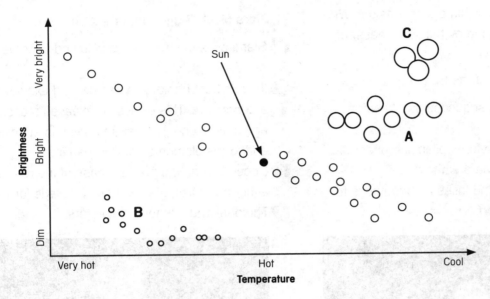

i) What type of star does the Sun become, shown at position A?

.... **(1 mark)**

ii) After millions of years this star becomes similar to those shown at position B. What type of star is this?

.... **(1 mark)**

(iii) Using the graph, describe the two key features of each type of star.

Star A : ....

Star B : .... **(2 marks)**

(iv) What is the name of the star at the end of the Sun's life cycle?

.... **(1 mark)**

(b) A star that is much larger than our Sun takes a very different path. Part of its history takes it to position C shown in the diagram.

(i) What is the name for this type of star? .... **(1 mark)**

(ii) What is the name given to the catastrophic event that occurs eventually in these stars?

.... **(1 mark)**

(iii) What are the two possible final outcomes from such events?

....

.... **(2 marks)**

2 A skydiver jumps from an aeroplane and free falls without opening their parachute.

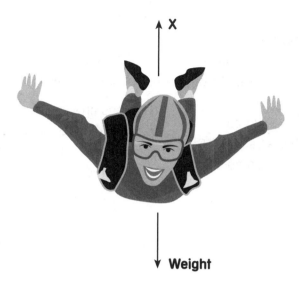

a) In the diagram of the free falling skydiver what is the name of the force X?

.... **(1 mark)**

b) Explain what happens to the force X as the skydiver accelerates.

.... **(1 mark)**

c) If the mass of the skydiver is 60kg, calculate their change in gravitational potential energy between leaving the aeroplane and falling 250m (take g = 10m/s²).

....

.... **(2 marks)**

d) In reality, not all the gravitational energy is converted into kinetic energy, however assuming that it is, calculate the speed of the skydiver after 250m of free fall.

....

....

.... **(3 marks)**

e) After 250m of free fall the skydiver no longer accelerates or speeds up. What do we call this point?

.... **(1 mark)**

f) What value does the force X now have at (and beyond) this point when the skydiver is still in free fall?

.... **(1 mark)**

P3 Medical Applications of Physics

X-rays

X-rays…
- form part of the **electromagnetic spectrum**
- have very short wavelengths of the same order of magnitude as the diameter of atoms and can cause **ionisation**
- are used in hospitals to diagnose and treat some medical conditions, e.g. bone fractures, dental problems, Computerised Tomography (CT) scans
- affect a photographic film in the same way as light
- can be detected using **charge-coupled devices (CCDs)** to form an image electronically.

The advantages for medical applications include:
- X-rays are transmitted by healthy tissue.
- X-rays are absorbed by metal and bone to produce shadow pictures.

CT scans produce two- and three-dimensional images. Although significantly more detail is obtained in CT images this is at a cost of increased levels of radiation dose to the patient.

Adequate protective screening, protective clothing and personal radiation detectors are used to monitor and limit exposure.

Ultrasound

Ultrasound are sound waves of frequencies greater than 20 000 Hz, i.e. beyond the upper limit of the hearing range for humans. Ultrasound waves are non-ionising

Electronic systems produce electrical oscillations, which are used to generate ultrasonic waves.

As ultrasonic waves pass from one medium or substance into another, they are partially reflected at the boundary. The time taken for these reflections is a measure of how far away the boundary is.

The distance between boundaries or interfaces can be determined by the equation:

$$s = v \times t$$

where s is the distance in metres (m), v is the speed in metres per second (m/s) and t is half the time taken for the pulse to leave the source, reflect off the boundary and return to the detector

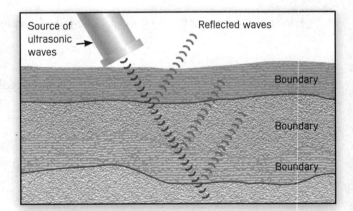

Ultrasound has many uses. Its uses in medicine include…
- pre-natal scanning
- imaging of damaged ligaments and muscles
- imaging of kidneys and destruction of kidney stones.

Reflection of Light

When light strikes a reflective surface it changes direction. This is called **reflection**.

The normal line is constructed perpendicular to the reflecting surface at the point of incidence. For reflected light the **angle of incidence (i)** is the same as the **angle of reflection (r)**.

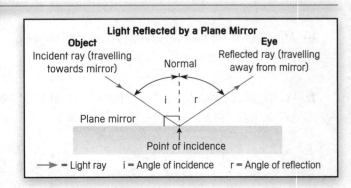

Key Words X-ray • CCD • Ultrasound • Reflection • Angle of incidence (i) • Angle of reflection (r)

Refraction of Light

When light crosses an interface (a boundary between two transparent media of different densities) it changes direction. This is called **refraction**. No refraction occurs when the light enters the interface at 90°, i.e. along the normal.

The **refractive index** is a property of transparent media and can be determined using the equation:

$$\text{Refractive Index} = \frac{\sin i}{\sin r}$$ where *sin i* and *sin r* are the sine values of the **angles** of **incidence** and **refraction**.

The refractive index of air is 1.0, water is 1.33 and glass is 1.5.

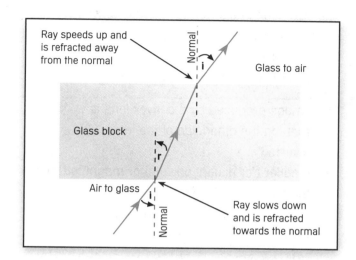

Converging and Diverging Lenses

A lens is a specially shaped piece of transparent material that refracts light. There are principally two types of lenses:

- **Converging lens (convex lens)** – thickest at the centre and represented by ↕ in ray diagrams.
- **Diverging lens (concave lens)** – thinnest at the centre and represented by ⑃ in ray diagrams.

The shape of the lens determines its **curvature**, i.e. how much a light ray is refracted through it. A light ray that enters a lens at its centre is undeviated. This line is called the **principal axis** of the lens.

In a convex lens light from an object is refracted **inwards** at the two curved surfaces of the lens so that they meet at a point called the **focus** or **focal point** (F). This is on the **opposite** side of the lens to the object and is **real**.

In a concave lens the focus appears to come from a point on the **same** side as the object and is not real, i.e. **virtual**.

The distance between the centre of the lens and the focus (real or virtual) is called the **focal length** (f). For **parallel rays** of light the focal point lies on the **principal axis**.

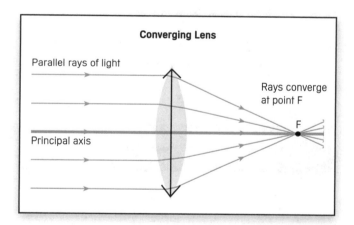

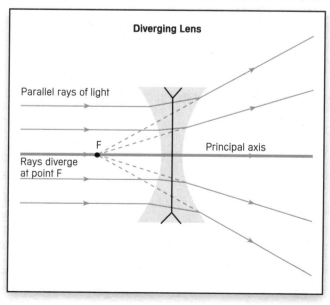

Images Produced by Lenses

The size of an image produced by a convex or concave lens depends on the distance of the object from the lens.

Convex Lens	Concave Lens
The image produced by a convex lens is... <ul><li>**real** (on the other side of the lens)</li><li>**inverted**</li><li>**smaller** (for distant objects) or **magnified** (when the object is between 'F' and '2F').</li></ul> 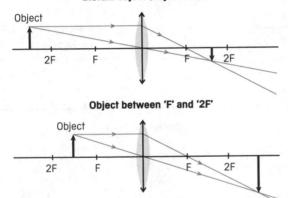	The image produced by a concave lens is... <ul><li>**virtual** (on the same side as the object)</li><li>**upright** (not inverted).</li></ul> 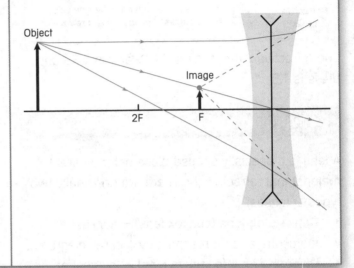

Magnification and Focal Length

The **magnification** of a lens can be calculated using the equation:

$$\text{Magnification} = \frac{\text{Image height}}{\text{Object height}}$$

The magnification of a lens has no units, i.e. it is just a number. A converging lens can be used as a magnifying glass.

The focal length of a lens is determined by...
- the **refractive index** of the material from which the lens is made
- the **curvature** of the two surfaces of the lens.

(HT) For a given focal length, the greater the refractive index the flatter the lens (i.e. thinner).

Quick Test

1. Name two ways in which X-rays can be detected.
2. Give two examples of ultrasound used in medicine.
3. What is the name given to the phenomenon when light enters a converging or diverging lens to form an image?
4. If the image height is 4.2cm and the object height only 0.7cm, calculate the magnification of the lens.

The Structure of the Eye

The eye receives light and sends this information to the brain via the optic nerve, which interprets the image.

The main components of the eye are shown in the diagram.

The **cornea** refracts most of the light whilst the **pupil** (opening in the **iris**) adjusts the light intensity. The **lens** provides further refraction before the image is formed on the light-sensitive **retina**. The **optic nerve** carries this information to the brain.

The ciliary muscles control the shape of the eye lens. This allows light from objects at different distances to be brought into focus.

The eye can focus on objects between the **near point** (approximately 25cm) and the **far point** (infinity).

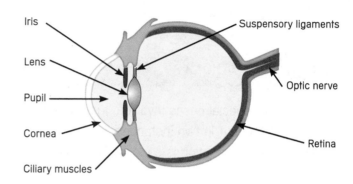

Eye Defects

There are two types of defective vision:
- **Long sight** caused by the eyeball being too short and unable to focus on near objects.
- **Short sight**, caused by the eyeball being too long and unable to focus on distant objects.

Both long sight and short sight can be corrected by using **glasses**, which adjust the light before entering the eye to allow it to focus correctly. Glasses are made from concave lenses, convex lenses or a combination of both lenses.

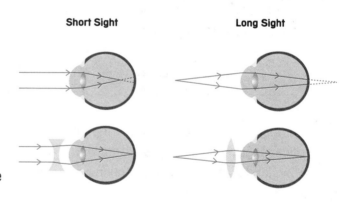

Short Sight   **Long Sight**

Camera and Magnifying Glass

Unlike the eye, both a **camera** and a **magnifying** glass have **fixed converging lenses** with definite focal lengths.

A magnifying glass enlarges an object size if the distance from the object to the lens is less than the focal length. The image is…
- **virtual**
- **upright**
- **enlarged**.

A converging lens in a camera produces an image on film or via a CCD. These are equivalent to the retina in the eye.

A convex lens magnifies when the object is between the focal point 'F' and the centre of the lens.

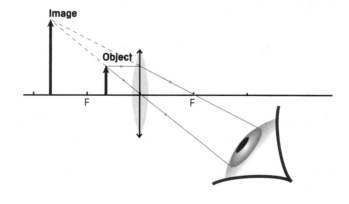

P3 Medical Applications of Physics

Power of a Lens

The **power of a lens** is determined by its focal length using the equation:

$$P = \frac{1}{f}$$

where P is the power in dioptres (D) and f is the focal length in metres (m)

The power of a...
- **converging lens** is **positive** (real focal point)
- **diverging lens** is **negative** (virtual focal point).

The Critical Angle

There are two special cases involving the refraction of light, which occur in two instances:

1. The angle of refraction is equal to 90°. The light ray travels on the boundary between glass and air. The angle of incidence is then called the **critical angle** (c).

(HT) The critical angle can also be used to determine the refractive index using the equation:

$$\text{Refractive index} = \frac{1}{\sin c}$$

2. The angle of incidence is greater than the critical angle. In this case **total internal reflection** takes place. No refraction occurs so no light escapes from the glass.

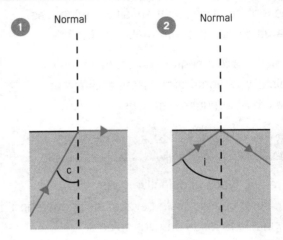

Medical **endoscopes** use the principle of total internal reflection to 'see' inside the body. Visible light is sent down thin, flexible glass rods, called **optical fibres** that are inserted into the body. The image is returned along the same fibres to an eye-piece or camera.

Lasers

A **laser** is a device that amplifies light to produce a very **intense** and very **narrow** beam. The word 'laser' means Light Amplification by Stimulated Emission of Radiation. Lasers can be made from solids, liquids or gases. Modern **devices** are very **small** and **compact**.

Lasers are used in **eye surgery**, for example...
- to repair damaged retinas
- to **remove diseased or damaged cells** by **cutting**, **cauterising** or **burning** the tissue.

Optical fibres are used to guide the laser beam to the correct area of the body.

Quick Test

1. What action do the ciliary muscles have within the eye?
2. What is the normal range of vision of the human eye?
3. What is meant by 'critical angle'?
4. 'Total internal reflection' is used in optical fibres. What is total internal reflection?
5. Give an example of where total internal reflection has been applied.

Key Words   Power of a lens • Critical angle • Total internal reflection • Optical fibre • Laser

Centre of Mass

The **centre of mass** (C of M) of an object is the point through which the **whole mass** of the **object** is considered to act. It can be thought of as the point where all the mass is concentrated.

For example, if you balance an object on the end of your finger, the centre of mass of the object is the point at which the object **balances**. The centre of mass of **symmetrical objects** is found easily by finding the intersection of the **axes of symmetry**.

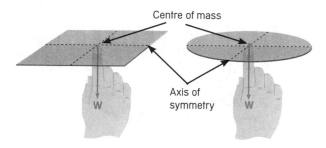

Centre of mass

Axis of symmetry

For thin, irregular shaped materials, with no lines of symmetry, the centre of mass can be found by using a simple plumb line. A suspended object will always come to rest with its centre of mass directly **below** the point of suspension.

Objects with a wide base and a low centre of mass, e.g. Bunsen burners, are more stable than those objects with a narrow base and a high centre of mass, e.g. ladders.

The following method can be used:

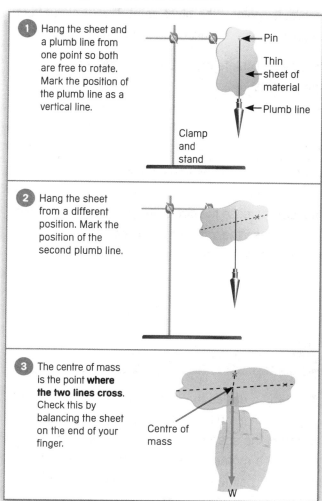

1 Hang the sheet and a plumb line from one point so both are free to rotate. Mark the position of the plumb line as a vertical line.

Pin

Thin sheet of material

Plumb line

Clamp and stand

2 Hang the sheet from a different position. Mark the position of the second plumb line.

3 The centre of mass is the point **where the two lines cross**. Check this by balancing the sheet on the end of your finger.

Centre of mass

W

The Pendulum

A mass at the end of a piece of string that oscillates back and forth gives an example of a simple pendulum. The number of times the mass swings back and forth every second gives its **frequency** of oscillation.

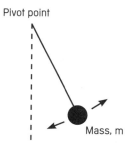

Pivot point

Mass, m

For a simple pendulum there is a connection between the time period and frequency given by:

$$T = \frac{1}{f}$$

where T is the time period in seconds (s) and f is the frequency in hertz (Hz)

The **time period**, T, only depends on the **length** of the pendulum and not on the mass.

Simple applications of this effect are seen in children's **playground rides** and in **fairgrounds**.

Moments

Forces can be used to turn objects about a particular point – the **pivot point**. The turning effect of such a force is called the **moment**.

You can calculate the size of a moment by using the formula:

$$M = F \times d$$

where M is the moment of the force in newton-metres (Nm), F is the force in newtons (N) and d is the perpendicular distance from the line of action of the force to the pivot in metres (m)

You can increase the size of the moment in two ways:
- **Increase** the value of the **force**.
- **Increase** the perpendicular **distance**.

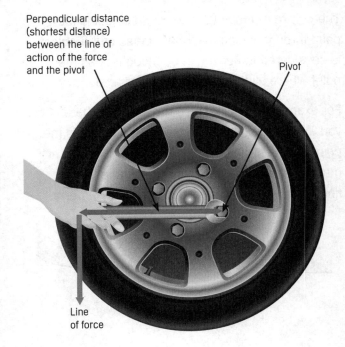

Perpendicular distance (shortest distance) between the line of action of the force and the pivot

Pivot

Line of force

Levers

A **lever** is a device that acts like a **force multiplier** or a distance multiplier. For example, doubling the length of the spanner to undo a wheel nut will either double the moment of the force for the same force applied or half the force applied to maintain the same moment of the force.

The application of levers is numerous, but two examples include...
- lifting a wheelbarrow
- opening a tin of paint with a screwdriver.

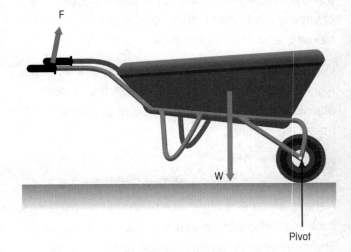

F

W

Pivot

Law of Moments

When an object isn't turning, there must be a balance between...
- the **total moments** of the forces turning the object in a **clockwise direction**
- the **total moments** of the forces turning the object in an **anticlockwise direction**.

Total clockwise moments	=	Total anticlockwise moments

This is called the **law of moments**.

Moment • Lever • Law of moments

HT Law of Moments

A plank is pivoted at its centre of mass and has two forces F_1 and F_2 pulling it downwards. The plank is balanced and not turning, so the total clockwise moment must equal the total anticlockwise moment.

$$F_1 \times d_1 = F_2 \times d_2$$

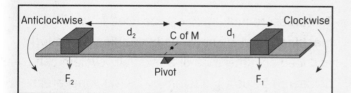

Example

A plank is pivoted at its centre of mass and has balanced forces acting. Calculate F_2.

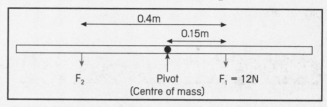

Total clockwise moments = Total anticlockwise moments

$$12N \times 0.15m = F_2 \times (0.4 - 0.15)m$$

$$\text{So, } F_2 = \frac{12N \times 0.15m}{0.25m}$$

$$= \textbf{7.2N}$$

HT Stability

An object will **topple** (fall over) if the **line of action of the force**, e.g. its **weight** lies **outside its base**. The **weight** of the object causes a **turning effect**, which makes the object topple.

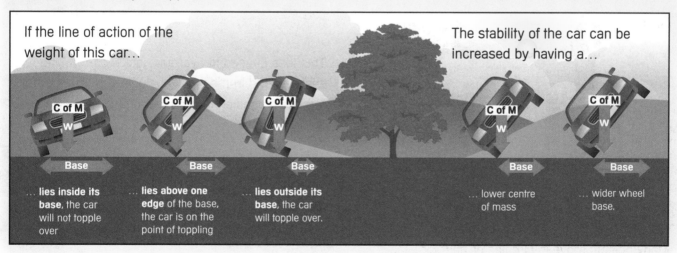

If the line of action of the weight of this car…

…**lies inside its base**, the car will not topple over

…**lies above one edge** of the base, the car is on the point of toppling

…**lies outside its base**, the car will topple over.

The stability of the car can be increased by having a…

…lower centre of mass

…wider wheel base.

Quick Test

1. What does the centre of mass represent?
2. What is the position of the centre of mass of a rectangle 5cm long by 3cm wide?
3. An object has forces applied to it but it is not turning. What can be said about the moments on the object?
4. What happens when the line of action of the weight of a car lies outside its base?

Pressure

Pressure is the **force** that acts over a particular **surface area**. A force acting over a small area gives a larger pressure than the same force acting over a bigger area.

The formula for pressure is:

$$P = \frac{F}{A}$$

where P is the pressure in pascals (Pa), F is the force in newtons (N) and A is the cross-sectional area in metres squared (m^2). 1 Pa is the same as $1 N/m^2$

Hydraulic Systems

Liquids are virtually incompressible, and the **pressure** in a liquid is transmitted **equally** in **all directions**. This means that a force exerted at one point on a liquid will be transmitted to other points in the liquid.

The pressure in a **liquid** can be used to **work machinery** and is known as **hydraulics**. The effort and load on either side of a hydraulic system can be altered by using different cross-sectional areas. This enables the system to be used as a force multiplier.

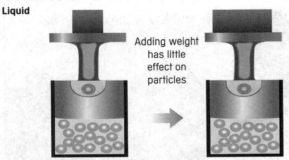

Gas

Adding weight compresses gas particles

Liquid

Adding weight has little effect on particles

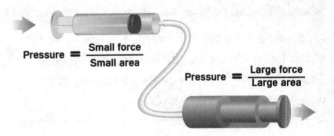

Pressure $= \dfrac{\text{Small force}}{\text{Small area}}$

Pressure $= \dfrac{\text{Large force}}{\text{Large area}}$

This idea is used in hydraulic jacks, car braking systems and in mechanical diggers, where a small force is magnified to produce a much larger force at the critical point.

Motion in a Circle

Many objects move in circular, or near circular paths. For example...

- a conker spun on a piece of string
- spinning rides in fairgrounds
- the London Eye
- cars going around corners
- spin driers in washing machines
- satellites orbiting the Earth
- planets orbiting the Sun.

Pressure • Incompressible • Hydraulics

Centripetal Force

Any object moving with a constant speed in a circular path is **continuously accelerating** towards the centre of the circle.

When there is a change in **velocity** there is an **associated acceleration**. This is because the **direction** of motion is continuously **changing**, not the speed.

The resultant force causing this acceleration is called the centripetal force. This force is always **directed towards the centre of the circle**, i.e. inwards.

The centripetal force may be provided by…
- friction, e.g. a car's wheels on the road surface as the car is turning
- tension, e.g. a conker spun on a piece of string.

The centripetal force needed to make an object perform circular motion increases by…
- **increasing the mass** of the object
- **increasing the speed** of the object
- **decreasing the radius** of the circle.

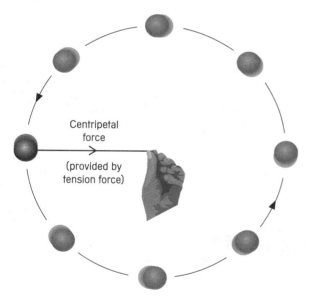

Centripetal force

(provided by tension force)

Quick Test

1. What is the unit of pressure?
2. What is used to transmit the force in a hydraulic system?
3. An athlete is undergoing rotational movement just before he throws a hammer. What provides the centripetal force causing the hammer to accelerate in this way?
4. In circular motion at constant speed why is there a centripetal acceleration?

The Motor Effect

When a current flows through a wire a **magnetic field** is produced around the wire. This **electromagnetic effect** is used…

- on cranes for lifting iron and steel
- in circuit breakers
- in loudspeakers
- in electric bells.

When a wire (conductor) carrying a current is placed in an **external magnetic field**, the **magnetic field formed around the wire** interacts with this permanent magnetic field. This causes the **wire** to experience a force that makes it **move**. This is called the motor effect.

Creating a Current

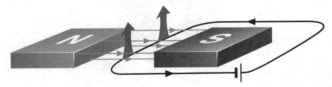

But, the wire will **not experience a force** if it's **parallel** to the **magnetic field**.

The size of the force on the wire can be increased by…

- **increasing the size of the current** (e.g. having more cells)

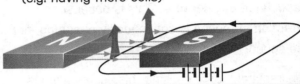

- **increasing the strength** of the **magnetic field** (e.g. having stronger magnets).

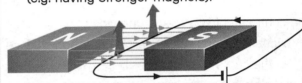

The direction of the force on the wire can be reversed by…

- reversing the **direction of flow** of the current (e.g. turning the cell around)

- reversing the **direction of the magnetic field** (e.g. swapping the magnets around).

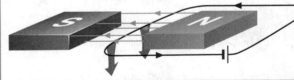

Fleming's Left-hand Rule

The direction of the force can be identified using **Fleming's left-hand rule**:

- The **F**irst finger points in the direction of the magnetic **F**ield.
- The se**C**ond finger points in the direction of the **C**urrent.
- The thu**M**b points in the direction of the **M**ovement.

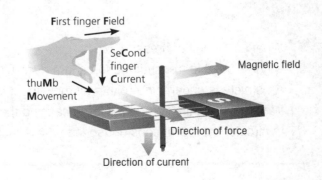

First finger **F**ield

Se**C**ond finger **C**urrent

thu**M**b **M**ovement

Magnetic field

Direction of force

Direction of current

Electromagnetic Induction

Electromagnetic induction uses **movement** to produce a **current**. Generators use this effect to produce electricity.

If a conducting wire, or coil of wires, is moved through or 'cuts' through a magnetic field, a potential difference (p.d.) is induced across the ends of the wire. If the coil of wire forms part of a complete circuit, an electrical current will be induced.

If there is no movement, then no current flows.

The same effect is obtained if the coil of wire is stationary and the magnetic field is moved. We call this current an **induced** current.

Induced currents are used in a bicycle dynamo.

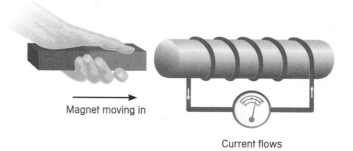

Magnet moving in

Current flows

No movement

No current

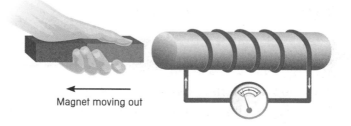

Magnet moving out

Current flows opposite way

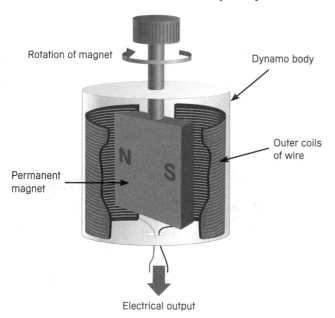

Rotation of magnet

Dynamo body

Outer coils of wire

Permanent magnet

N   S

Electrical output

Potential Difference

The size of the potential difference, and hence the current, can be increased by...

- increasing the **speed** of the **movement** of the magnet or coils
- increasing the **strength** of the **magnetic field**
- increasing the **number of turns** on the coil.

Quick Test

1. **a)** What is produced when a current flows through a conducting wire in a magnetic field?
   b) Give two examples of where this effect has been applied.
2. A loop of conducting wire carrying a current crosses an external magnetic field at 90°. What effect is observed?
3. Briefly describe Fleming's left-hand rule.

Transformers

A **transformer** changes electrical energy from one potential difference to another potential difference. Transformers are made up of two coils, called the **primary** and **secondary coils**, wrapped around a soft iron core.

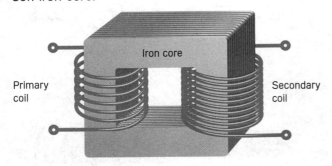

Primary coil

Iron core

Secondary coil

An **alternating potential difference** across the primary coil causes an **alternating current** to flow (input). This alternating current creates a continuously changing magnetic field in the iron core, which induces an **alternating potential difference** across the ends of the secondary coil (output).

The **potential difference** across the primary and secondary coils of a transformer are related by the equation:

$$\frac{V_p}{V_s} = \frac{n_p}{n_s}$$

where V_p is the potential difference across the primary coil in volts (V), V_s is the potential difference across the secondary coil in volts (V), n_p is the number of turns on the primary coil and n_s is the number of turns on the secondary coil

For example, a transformer has 200 turns on the primary coil and 800 turns on the secondary coil. If a potential difference of 230V is applied to the primary coil, the potential difference across the secondary coil can be determined using the equation above.

$$\frac{230}{V_s} = \frac{200}{800}$$

$$V_s = \textbf{920V}$$

Step-up and Step-down Transformers

A **step-up transformer** has more turns in the secondary coil than the primary coil. The potential difference across the secondary coil is **greater** than that across the primary coil.

A **step-down transformer** has fewer turns in the secondary coil than the primary coil. The potential difference across the secondary coil is less than that across the primary coil.

Step-up and step-down transformers are used in the **National Grid** to ensure the efficient transmission of electricity.

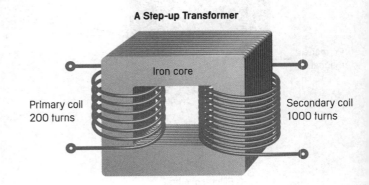

A Step-up Transformer

Iron core

Primary coil
200 turns

Secondary coil
1000 turns

A Step-down Transformer

Iron core

Primary coil
1000 turns

Secondary coil
200 turns

Transforming Efficiency

If transformers were assumed to be 100% efficient, the electrical power output would equal the electrical power input (see power, p40). This can be stated using the equation:

$$V_p \times I_p = V_s \times I_s$$

where V_p is the potential difference across the primary coil in volts (V),
I_p is the current in the primary coil in amperes (amps, A),
V_s is the potential difference across the secondary coil in volts (V)
I_s is the current in the secondary coil in amperes (amps, A)

Switch Mode Transformers

Switch mode transformers are much lighter and smaller than traditional transformers and operate at a much **higher frequency**, often between **50kHz and 200kHz**. They operate using the 50Hz mains supply.

Switch mode transformers use very little power when they are switched on, as no load is applied.

They have found useful applications as chargers for…

* **mobile phones**
* **digital cameras**
* **computer laptops**.

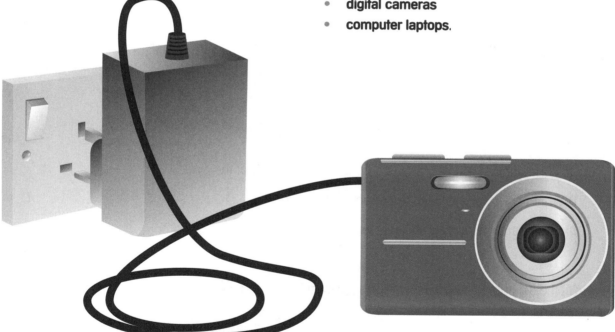

Quick Test

1. What are the main components of a transformer?
2. Do transformers use a direct current or an alternating current?
3. Give two advantages of switch mode transformers over traditional transformers.
4. Over what frequency range do switch mode transformers work?
5. Give an example of the application of switch mode transformers.

1 There are two main eye defects, know as short sighted and long sighted, which can be readily corrected.

a) i) Briefly describe the condition of a person who is long sighted.

....

.... **(1 mark)**

ii) This condition is caused by a lack of movement in the eye lens. What controls the shape of the eye lens?

....

.... **(1 mark)**

b) On the diagram below draw two light rays, from the common point shown just in front of the eye, one above and one below the dashed line given, to show the effects of a person who is long sighted.

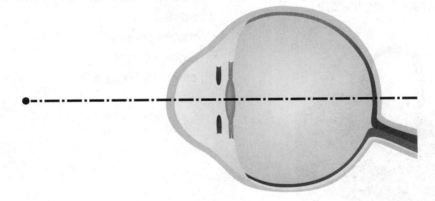

(3 marks)

c) To correct this eye defect a lens can be placed in front of the eye.

i) What type of lens is used to correct for long sight?... **(1 mark)**

ii) What effect does the additional lens have in correcting this defect?

.... **(1 mark)**

d) On the diagram below draw two light rays from the common point in front of the eye to show the effects of using the lens illustrated.

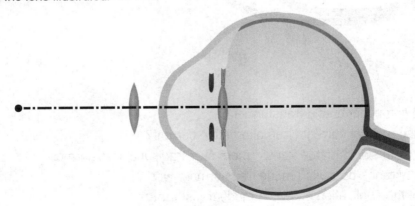

(3 marks)

2 The diagram below shows a coil of wire located between the poles of a magnet.

The arrows indicate the direction of the conventional current.

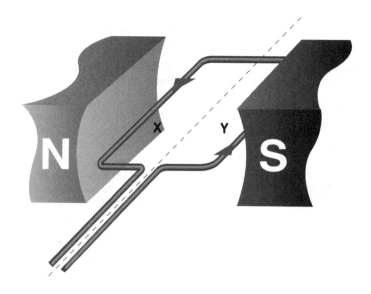

a) On the diagram draw arrows to show the direction of the force on sides **X** and **Y** on the coil of wire.

(2 marks)

b) What rule is used to determine this direction?

.... **(1 mark)**

c) Explain why these forces cause the coil to rotate.

....

.... **(2 marks)**

d) What is the name given to this effect?

.... **(1 mark)**

e) What would happen to the coil if the magnets were swapped around?

.... **(1 mark)**

f) What two methods could be used to allow the coil to rotate faster about its axle?

....

.... **(2 marks)**

Answers

Unit 1

Quick Test Answers
Page 15
1. Infrared radiation
2. True
3. Regular or orderly pattern
4. The movement of fast-moving free electrons
5. **Any two from:** Amount of surface area of a material; A material's temperature; The air pressure
6. How effective a material is as an insulator
7. 42 000J

Page 17
1. It is wasted; Turns into heat; Warms the surroundings
2. 12.5%
3. An energy transfer diagram showing arrows that are proportional to the amount of energy involved in each process
4. **(a)** Joules or kilowatt-hours **(b)** watts or kilowatts
5. 200W
6. **(a)** 1.2kWh **(b)** 12p

Page 20
1. **Any two from:** Coal; Oil; Gas
2. Solid, liquid or gas obtained from lifeless or living biological material
3. **Advantages:** Free electricity; Lack of air pollution; Expensive to set up; Inefficient
   Disadvantages: Expensive; Inefficient
4. Prevents carbon dioxide build up in the atmosphere; Stored in old oil fields or gas fields
5. High voltage reduces current and hence minimises energy loss
6. Converts the potential difference on the overhead cables to a safe level of 230V for consumers, e.g. houses

Page 23
1. Yes
2. The maximum or minimum height (disturbance) of a wave from the midpoint.

3. Upright, same size, virtual and laterally inverted
4. Longitudinal
5. Between 20Hz and 20 000Hz
6. It is expanding; It started off from a very small initial point (Big Bang)

Exam Practice Answers
Pages 24–25
1. **a)** m is the mass (in kg); c is the specific thermal capacity (in J/kg°C), θ is the change in temperature (°C)
   b) $E = mc\theta = 0.6 \times 4200 \times (100 - 20)$
   $E = 201600J$ or $\approx 202kJ$ (*1 mark for correct substitution into equation and 1 mark for answer*)
   c) (i) Using $E = Pt$ and rearranging gives $t = \frac{E}{p} = \frac{201600}{1.7 \times 10^3} = 118.6s \approx 2$ min
   (*1 mark for correct substitution into equation and 1 mark for answer*)
   (ii) $t = \frac{2}{60} = 0.033$hrs
   d) $E = Pt = 1.7$kW x 0.033hrs; $= 0.057$kWh
   e) Cost $= 0.057$kWh $\times$ 10p $= 0.57$p

2. **a)** A 2; B 3; C 1
   b)
   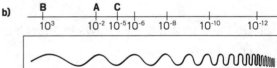
   c) $v = f\lambda$ and hence $\lambda = \frac{v}{f}$; $= \frac{330}{2000} = 0.165$m
   d) Sound waves need a medium to travel in; Water molecules are closer together than air molecules; Sound waves are therefore transmitted through the material at a faster rate.

Unit 2

Quick Test Answers
Page 31
1. An acceleration in the direction of the resultant force
2. Direction
3. Negative gradient or slope
4. Friction force and driving force
5. Reaction time (thinking distance) and braking distance
6. Constant speed reached when the upward resistive force balances the downward force (weight)
7. $R = W$ or $R = mg$ at terminal velocity
8. Elastic potential energy

Page 33
1. Energy transferred
2. Power
3. 72 000J
4. Total momentum before = Total momentum after

Page 37
1. Repel
2. Current
3. Ohms or Ω
4. It is shared equally between the components
5. Decreases

Page 40
1. Fuse; RCCB
2. Green and yellow
3. 13A fuse
4. 3 coulombs

Page 44
1. M is the mass number – the number of protons and neutrons; A represents the atomic number – the number of protons.
2. A helium nucleus or 2 protons and 2 neutrons
3. Gamma radiation; Carries no charge and is not deflected by a magnetic field
4. The time taken for half of the radioactive nuclei to decay into stable nuclei

Page 47
1. Uranium-235 or plutonium-239
2. Neutrons released from the initial reaction go on to interact with other nuclei producing even more neutrons each time.
3. Within stars
4. Iron

Unit 2 (Cont.)

Exam Practice Answers
Pages 48–49
1. **a)** **i)** Red giant
    ii) White dwarf
    iii) Star A: brighter, cooler; Star B: dimmer, hotter
    iv) Black dwarf
    (b) **i)** Red super giant
    ii) Supernova explosions
    iii) Neutron star; Black hole

2. **a)** Air resistance / drag
    b) X becomes larger
    c) $E_p = mgh = 60 \times 10 \times 250; = 150000J$
    d) $E_k = \frac{1}{2}mv^2 = 150000J; v^2 = 2 \times \frac{150000}{60} = 5000;$
    so that $v = \sqrt{5000} \approx 71m/s$
    e) Terminal velocity
    f) 600N

Unit 3

Quick Test Answers
Page 52
1. Photographic film; CCD
2. **Any two from:** Pre-natal scanning; Imaging damaged ligaments and muscles; Imaging kidneys; Removal of kidney stones
3. Refraction
4. Six

Page 54
1. They control the shape of the lens
2. 25cm to infinity
3. The angle of refraction is directed along the boundary or at 90° to the normal
4. When a ray of light remains within a material by repeated reflection
5. In medical endoscopes

Page 57
1. A point at which all the mass is said to be concentrated
2. (2.5cm, 1.5cm) from any corner, or along the axes of symmetry
3. Total clockwise moment = Total anticlockwise moment
4. The car will topple over

Page 59
1. Pa or N/m²
2. Liquids
3. The tension in the wire
4. The velocity of the object changes because its direction changes and acceleration is the rate of change of velocity.

Page 61
1. **a)** A magnetic field is produced around the wire
    b) **Any two from:** Cranes for lifting iron; Circuit breakers; Electric bell; Loudspeaker; Electric relay
2. The wire experiences a force and moves
3. Thumb points in the direction of the movement, first finger points in the direction of the magnetic field, second finger points in direction of the current

Page 63
1. Soft iron core; Two coils (primary and secondary)
2. Alternating current
3. They are lighter; They are smaller
4. 50kHz to 200kHz
5. **Any one from:** Mobile phone chargers; Digital camera chargers; Laptop chargers

Exam Practice Answers
Pages 64–65
1. **a)** **i)** It is the inability to focus on near objects
    ii) The ciliary muscles
    b)

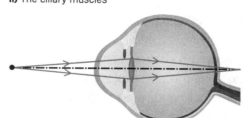

Two light rays must be drawn from the common point; They must show refraction at the lens; They must focus beyond the retina
    c) **i)** A converging lens or convex lens
    ii) It refracts the light before it enters the eye
    d)

Addition of a convex lens; Light rays showing refraction; Light rays focused on retina
2. **a)** Arrows should be drawn showing that side X moves up and side Y moves down
    b) Fleming's left-hand rule
    c) The coil of wire is on a spindle and the forces produce a moment or turning force; This makes the coil rotate about the spindle axle
    d) The motor effect
    e) The direction of motion would be reversed
    f) **Any two from:** Increase the size of the current; Increase the strength of the magnetic field; More turns

Glossary

Acceleration – the rate of change of velocity; units of m/s²; $a = \frac{F}{m}$

Alpha particle – a helium nucleus; 2 protons and 2 neutrons

Alternating current (a.c.) – an electric current that reverses its direction of flow repeatedly

Amplitude – the maximum disturbance/vibration measured from mid point

Angle of incidence (i) – the angle between a ray falling on a plane surface and the normal line at that point

Angle of reflection (r) – the angle between a reflected ray leaving a plane surface and the normal line at that point

Atom – the smallest part of an element; the building blocks of matter

Atomic number – the number of protons in an atom

Background radiation – radiation that is around us; predominantly from natural sources

Beta particle – an electron emitted from the nucleus

Big Bang – the massive explosion that sent all matter outwards signalling the start of the Universe creating time and space

Biofuel – a solid, liquid or gas obtained from lifeless or living biological material

Black dwarf – the end point in a star's life cycle for stars similar in mass to the Sun

Black hole – the remains of a star after a supernova explosion

Centre of mass – the point at which an object's mass is apparently concentrated

Centripetal force – the external force required to make an object follow a circular path at constant speed

Chain reaction – a reaction that is self-sustaining

Charge – a property of elementary particles; comes in two forms – positive and negative

Charge-coupled device (CCD) – a type of microchip that converts light into an electrical signal that is then used to form an image

Ciliary muscles – group of muscles in the eye that control the size of the lens

Circuit breaker – a safety device that automatically breaks an electric circuit when it becomes overloaded

Condensation – the change of a vapour into a liquid accompanied by heat transfer

Conduction – the energy transfer in solids without the substance itself moving

Conductor – a material that readily transfers energy by atom vibration or electrical energy through the movement of free electrons

Conservation of momentum – the total momentum before and after a collision is the same

Convection – the energy transfer through movement in liquids and gases

Converging (convex) lens – a lens in which light rays passing through it are refracted towards a central point

Cosmic Microwave Background Radiation (CMBR) – electromagnetic radiation that fills the entire Universe; remnant of the Big Bang

Critical angle – the angle of incidence that refracts a ray of light at 90° to the normal

Current (electric) – the rate of flow of electric charge; units of amperes (amps) A; $I = \frac{Q}{t}$

Current–potential difference graph – graph used to show how the current through a component varies with the potential difference across it

Diode – an electrical device that allows electric current to flow in one direction

Direct current (d.c) – an electric current that flows in one direction

Distance–time graph – a graph showing the distance travelled against time taken; the gradient of the line represents speed

Diverging (concave) lens – a lens in which light rays passing through it are refracted away from a virtual central point

Doppler effect – the change in wavelength or frequency associated with a moving source

Double insulated – electrical appliances that need no earth connection

Echo – a reflected sound wave

Efficiency – the ratio of energy (useful power) output to total energy (power) input, expressed as a percentage or as a decimal number

Elastic – a force applied to an object that recovers its original shape when the force is removed

Elastic potential energy – the energy stored in a stretched spring

Electrical energy – energy of electrical charge or current; measured in joules (J)

Electromagnetic induction – the induced current in a wire as it moves through a magnetic field

Electron – a fundamental particle with a charge of -1; orbits the nucleus

Energy transfer – a measure of how much work is done on an object or material

Enlarged – bigger than original size

Evaporation – the change from liquid into a vapour below the boiling point of the liquid

Fleming's left-hand rule – shows the connection between the directions of magnetic field, current and movement

Focal length – the distance between the lens centre and the focal point along the principal axis

Focus – any point through which rays of light converge

Fossil fuel – a fuel formed in the ground over millions of years from the remains of dead plants and animals

Force – a push or pull acting on an object

Frequency – the number of cycles or oscillations that occur in 1 second; measured in hertz (Hz)

Friction – a resistive force acting between two surfaces

Fuse – a thin wire that overheats and melts when overloaded to break an electric circuit; comes with different ratings

Gamma radiation – high energy, high frequency electromagnetic radiation

Gravitational field strength – the value of 'g' at a particular height above the Earth's surface

Gravitational potential energy – the energy that an object has due to its position in a gravitational field; $E_p = m \times g \times h$; units of joule (J)

Half-life – the average time taken for half of the unstable atoms in a radioactive material to decay

Hydraulics – mechanical systems involving the use of incompressible liquids or fluids

Incompressible – applied to liquids and fluids where the internal forces are the same throughout the substance

Infrared radiation – the transfer of thermal radiation by electromagnetic waves

Insulator – a material that doesn't conduct well

Ion – an atom that has gained or lost an electron

Ionising power – the ability of particles or electromagnetic radiation to ionise other neutral atoms or molecules

Isotopes – atoms of the same element that contain a different number of neutrons, but the same number of protons

Kinetic energy – the energy possessed by an object due to its motion: $E_k = \frac{1}{2} \times m \times v^2$; units of joule (J)

Kinetic theory – a theory that explains the physical properties of matter in terms of the movement of particles

Laser – light amplification by stimulated emission of radiation

Law of moments – when the total clockwise motion and total anticlockwise motion of an object are equal

Lever – a simple device that provides mechanical advantage of movement

Long sight – the inability of the eye to focus on near objects

Longitudinal wave – a wave where the oscillations are parallel to the direction of energy transfer

Magnification – the ratio of image size (height) over object size (height)

Main sequence – the position of a star that determines its life cycle; based on a star's mass

Mass number – the number of protons and neutrons in an atomic nucleus

Moment – a turning force; the product of the force and the perpendicular distance from the force to the pivot point

Momentum – a fundamental quantity that is a measure of the state of motion of an object; product of mass and velocity; $p = m \times v$; units of kg m/s

Motor effect – the movement of a conducting wire in a magnetic field

National Grid – a network of power lines and cables that carries electricity from the power station to the consumer

Nebula – a general term for a 'fuzzy' patch of sky composed of interstellar dust and gas

Neutron – a subatomic particle found in the nucleus; has no charge

Neutron star – the remains of a star after a supernova explosion

Non-renewable energy source – an energy source that can't be replaced as fast as it is used

Normal line – the line constructed at 90° to the reflecting surface at the point of incidence

Nuclear fission – the splitting of an atomic nucleus into two smaller nuclei with the emission of neutrons and energy

Glossary

Nuclear fuels – uranium and plutonium used in nuclear power stations to provide the transfer of energy by heat

Nuclear fusion – the joining together of light atomic nuclei with the emission of energy; main energy process in stars

Optical fibre – a thin strand of glass or plastic that uses total internal reflection to carry light

Potential difference – the energy transfer by unit charge passing from one point to another; measured in volts (V)

Power – work done or energy transferred in a given time; units of watts (W); $P = \frac{E}{t}$ and $P = I \times V$

Power of a lens – a measure of the ability of a lens to refract light; $P = \frac{1}{\text{focal length}}$

Pressure – force per unit area; $P = \frac{F}{A}$; units of Pascals (Pa)

Principal axis – the line passing through the centre of a lens

Proton – a subatomic particle found in the nucleus; has a charge of +1

Protostar – the initial gas and dust that forms a star

Radioactive – the decay of unstable nuclei by the emission of alpha or beta particles or gamma radiation

Red giant – part of a star's life cycle after leaving the main sequence for stars with masses similar to our Sun's mass

Red super giant – part of a star's life cycle after leaving the main sequence for stars with masses much larger than our Sun

Red-shift – the shift in light or other electromagnetic waves to longer wavelengths

Reflection – a change in direction of a wave when striking a plane surface

Refraction – the change in direction (and speed) of a wave as it passes from one medium to another

Refractive index – a measure of the ability of a material to refract light given by the ratio of the sine values of the angles of incidence and refraction; also given by $\frac{1}{\sin (\text{critical angle})}$

Renewable energy source – an energy source that can be replaced faster than it is used

Residual Current Circuit Breaker (RCCB) – automatic device for breaking a circuit; based on detecting a difference in current between live and neutral wires

Resistance – opposition to the flow of electric current; units of ohms

Resistor – an electrical device that resists the flow of an electric current

Resultant force – the combined effect of all forces acting on an object

Sankey diagram – an energy transfer diagram where the widths of the arrows are proportional to the amount of energy used

Short sight – the inability of the eye to focus on distant objects

Sound wave – forward and backward vibrations within a material or medium; sound waves are longitudinal waves; can't travel through a vacuum

Specific heat capacity – the amount of energy required to change the temperature of 1kg of a material by 1°C; measured in J/kg°C

Speed – the rate at which an object moves

Spring constant – the gradient of the line of a graph of force against extension; units of N/m

Static electricity – the loss or gain of electrons on the surface of a material

Stopping distance – the sum of the thinking distance and braking distance

Supernova – catastrophic explosion of a red super giant

Switch mode transformer – a small, light transformer that operates at frequencies between 50kHz and 200kHz

Tension – a resistive force in a wire or string

Terminal velocity – the constant maximum velocity reached by a falling object; weight balances the frictional forces

Thermal radiation – the transfer of infrared radiation; does not involve particles

Thermistor – a resistor whose resistance varies with temperature

Total internal reflection – the internal reflection of light achieved when the angle of incidence is greater than the critical angle

Transformer – an electrical device used to change the voltage or potential difference of alternating currents

Transverse wave – a wave where the oscillations are perpendicular to the direction of energy transfer

U-value – a measure of the effectiveness of a material as an insulator

Ultrasound – high frequency sound waves beyond the range of human hearing, i.e. 20 000Hz

Unstable nuclei – nuclei that are radioactive and emit radiation

Upright – an image that has the same orientation as the object

Velocity – the speed of an object in a specified direction

Velocity–time graph – a graph showing velocity against time; the gradient of the line represents acceleration; the area under the line represents distance (displacement)

Virtual – an image from which the light rays appear to come from the object

Wave equation – an equation that connects frequency and wavelength for waves; $v = f \times \lambda$

Wavelength – the distance between two successive peaks or troughs in a wave

Weight – the gravitational force exerted on an object with mass; $W = m \times g$

White dwarf – part of a star's life cycle after its red giant stage

Work done – the product of force and distance moved; $W = F \times d$

X-ray – electromagnetic radiation of shorter wavelength than ultraviolet radiation

Index